Acclaim for *REPAIR Your Life*

"When we found the model for our women's support group, *The Lamplighters*, and the program *REPAIR*, we were thrilled. It is exactly what was desperately needed in International Falls and Koochiching County. We have now expanded our support group to include women of Fort Frances and the surrounding area in Ontario, Canada. After finding Marjorie McKinnon and the support she offered, we are now into our program. Our first meeting was a huge success. Thank you Marjorie and God bless you for adapting this program for our survivors to follow. You have given survivors hope to continue on their healing journey."

—Donna Gustafson, Executive Director,
Sunrise Center Against Sexual Abuse

"I just feel very touched this morning because I am reading your *REPAIR* book for adults. It is wonderful and is helping me in my work with DV survivors. I just want to tell you that you are an amazing woman and I want to thank you for sharing your story, life, and truth in this book. I feel honored to know you, and like you, am dedicated to helping other women have and find their voice."

—Monteze Deputy, Victim Advocate

"...a magnificent book, written with such understanding of the pain a child goes through and the gates that are needed to get through and enter in order to heal. Such love and thought go into this book of healing. I highly recommend it to anyone who has ever experienced this kind of abuse."

—Cheryl Newton-Boyer, Lamplighter Facilitator

"As a practicing Marriage and Family Therapist for almost twenty years in California, and as a recovering woman from the effects of childhood sexual abuse, I am delighted to write this letter of recommendation. Marjorie McKinnon's book, *REPAIR Your Life*, is logically constructed and sensitively presented. The author employs didactic and experiential learning in a clear manner, which invites the reader to risk dealing with the scars of childhood sexual abuse and incest.

REPAIR, when used as an adjunct to therapy and/or support groups, offers 'hands-on' exercises, which will facilitate and hasten the process of healing. I have personal experience with many of the tools the author presents and can attest to their usefulness. Anyone wanting to recover from the life-long trauma of childhood sexual abuse will benefit from this book. *REPAIR Your Life* will become the reader's wise and trusted companion along the road to wellness."

—Marcelle B. Taylor, MFT

D1591790

"As a counseling psychologist, who often works with people who had suffered sexual abuse as children, I find every recommendation in this book to be valid. This program just has to work, because, whether intuitively or through research, Marjorie McKinnon has assembled a highly effective program of recovery. Editing this book has been an honor. I hope it is read by all those many people who desperately need it."

—Robert Rich, PhD, www.BobsWriting.com

"If you or someone you care about is a survivor of childhood sexual abuse, this book should prove invaluable to your recovery. Most people realize that childhood sexual abuse is traumatic, but not everyone understands or recognizes the serious and often life-long effects.

The author of this valuable book, Marjorie McKinnon, has written extensively how survivors can work to move beyond the trauma of abuse. With hard work and patience, it can be done. She pulls no punches, and never trivializes the difficulty of dealing with this problem. She has set the program forward with a really useful acronym, REPAIR, to illustrate the steps a survivor and their friends and family or therapist needs to take to begin the process of healing. Written in a style that is very easy to understand and to follow, the survivor will work through 6 different steps to recovery.

Numerous therapists have recommended this process, and I believe it could be an invaluable tool both for professionals and caring friends and family members of survivors. Anyone wanting to move beyond the trauma of incest and childhood sexual abuse can find hope, healing and care within these pages. Information is also given about support groups and finding them, an invaluable resource that many people are unaware are available to them."

Lauri C. Coates, *ReviewTheBook.com*

"REPAIR is a recovery journey from childhood sexual abuse. I am a victim advocate and have used this book with survivors I work with. I never get tired of readers saying to me '.... this is so what I have been experiencing'. It is set up in such a way to let the reader go at their own pace. It details warning signs and it provides such incredible tools in a journey that otherwise is so dark and lonely. It truly is a miraculous book providing its readers with a glimpse of hope for the future."

Juanita Rasmusson
Grand Forks, North Dakota Area - Crime Victim Advocate
Executive Director at Norman County Victim Assistance Program

REPAIR
FOR TEENS

A Program for Recovery from
Incest & Childhood Sexual Abuse

by Marjorie McKinnon
Foreword by Sharon Wallace
Illustrations by Michal Splho

Library of Congress Cataloging-in-Publication Data

McKinnon, Margie, 1942-
 Repair for teens : a program for recovery from incest & childhood sexual abuse / Marjorie McKinnon ; illustrations by Michal Splho ; foreword by Sharon Wallace.
    p. cm.
 Includes index.
 ISBN 978-1-61599-127-3 (hardcover : alk. paper) -- ISBN 978-1-61599-126-6 (pbk. : alk. paper)
 1. Sexually abused children--Rehabilitation--Juvenile literature. 2. Incest victims--Rehabilitation--Juvenile literature. I. Splho, Michal, ill. II. Title.
 RJ507.S49M382 2012
 616.85'8360651--dc23
                                            2011048521

Published by:
Loving Healing Press
5145 Pontiac Trail
Ann Arbor, MI 48105
USA

http://www.LovingHealing.com or
info@LovingHealing.com
Fax +1 734 663 6861
Tollfree 888 761 6268

Distributed by Ingram Book Group (USA/CAN), New Leaf Distributing, Bertram's Books (UK)

Contents

Table of Figures

Foreword

I am an international public speaker, author, poet and—yes—a survivor of childhood emotional, physical, and sexual abuse. If I could have read a book like this one, *Repair For Teens* by Marjorie McKinnon, I am sure the dark road I travelled would have been easier to bear. Easier that is, by knowing I was not unique and not alone in my struggle from Victim to Victor.

In addition to McKinnon's unique REPAIR method, this book shows the Twelve-Step recovery program in a way that many of us can relate to. For instance, the Bridge of Recovery and having to cross it to heal made so much sense to me. I recognized some behavioral traits from the list given. This gave me insight into times when I have wondered why I sometimes react to certain things when other people don't:

> "You never walk alone until your legs are strong enough to hold you."

I have been able to identify with this sentence and I wish I had the forethought to know this many years ago. I remember feelings of guilt and loneliness through my childhood and sought only for my abuse to stop. At that time in my life, it never occurred to me that my abuser was actually breaking the law; he was just hurting me. I didn't have the expertise of knowing he was wrong; only that I was bad. I carried this *misplaced guilt* for many years afterward. Again, if I had access to books like *Repair For Teens*, I would have not felt so alone and isolated for many years.

Relating to others and knowing you are not alone with your pain, and that others suffered much like yourself when growing up, helps us to understand and accept our pain. This is a phenomenon I never expected, but is comforting to know now. Watching others speak out about this trauma and knowing we *can* heal is the most important thing for a survivor.

As a recovering teenager, who believed she was alone in her struggle, having access to this book would have made my pain less lonely. We might have no one to turn to when the very person hurting us is a family member, but we can seek help in the written word by others who have survived and thrived through the same emptiness and pain. I thoroughly recommend this title for anyone, young or old, who has lived through a childhood torn.

Sharon Wallace, author of *A House Full of Whispers* and
Surviving A House Full of Whispers

Introduction

I suffered incest at the hands of my father and recovered after many years of poor choices: abusive husbands, addictions, suicide attempts, time spent in psychiatric wards and a women's shelter. Several years ago, I realized that someone who had walked the same road could prove to be a sensitive and pragmatic resource for those who are trying to heal. I know so well what goes on inside the heart, the mind, and the soul of one who has been sexually abused as a child.

My program, REPAIR, is the result of several years of note-taking, journalizing, meditation, and piecing together parts of my own life, as well as conversations with other incest survivors across the country. As I worked my way through recovery, I kept notes in anticipation that someday what I was learning might help others. When I began this book, I re-read my own first-person account, *Let Me Hurt You and Don't Cry Out,* to re-walk the path I had taken. I never realized at the time how blessed I was; for that path, although rugged, was straight, and in retrospect provided me with invaluable help to create this program.

I met many incest survivors during my years of recovery, both locally and in traveling to other states. Every place I went, I talked about what I had gone through. It proved to be a catharsis. Initially, people were shocked that I spoke of what had happened so openly and as if it were not my fault. My comment, "It wasn't", at first proved startling. Little by little, I noticed that others came forward with their stories. Sometimes they spoke in hushed whispers, giving furtive looks, as if they feared punishment. At other times, they spoke boldly, trying to escape from a prison. When I asked questions and responded with sympathy, they became more daring—now giving details, now talking of feelings, often sharing about others they knew who had also survived abuse. I tracked coincidences, made notes on their needs and their pain, and asked questions about resources available in their areas and what it might take to help them feel whole again.

When I began the outline for the program, I knew that it cried out for a title that aptly described what needed to be done. "Repair" was the first word that came to my mind. It literally means to restore by replacing a part or putting together what is torn or broken; to restore to a sound or healthy state. What better word describes your goal in the case of childhood sexual abuse? In particular, I knew that it wasn't enough to rid yourself of the pain; you needed to fill the void with something good. I also knew that the ultimate reward was making healthy choices and living a life free from the despair that kept you bound by dark shadows, doomed to live in a three-sided prison.

After spending a year with my initial therapist, I was on my own. Although I eventually found another, most of my success in recovery was due to following my own instincts and wading through the trial and error of many different groups, seminars, books, and recordings. The techniques that I devised, some of which I had no idea at the time would contribute monumentally to getting healthy, were fine-tuned. Developing the stages came naturally as I thought back on what had happened during the five years that I was in both recovery and post recovery.

* * *

Most of us have learned ways over the years to cope with depression, emotional pain, and shadowy memories that bring anxiety. Some of you are saying, *I'm still angry, but my life is ok*. But is it? In this program, you're going to ask yourself some hard questions. Hopefully, by the end of it, you'll see things more clearly.

I want to say a word about those of you who are living at home and have been or are being victimized sexually by a family member. If they know you are working this program, it is going to make them feel as if they are losing their power, and they will not be happy about it. My recommendation is for you to read it and work the exercises somewhere other than in your home. If you can afford it, check into getting a Kindle, Nook or Kobo e-reader. My REPAIR books are all on these devices. That will give you the anonymity you need. If you have a school counselor, you might want to speak with them about your options. I will be talking about this frequently in this book. What they are doing is against the law. They can be arrested and go to prison. I know that the thought of exposing them is terrifying. You may not have the support of your mother (if she is not the perpetrator) or father (if he is not the perpetrator). You may have grandparents or a godparent that you trust you can talk to. It is important that you find someone who will be a loyal and trusting ally. It may take time for you to find the courage to expose them. If you called Child Protective Services, they would have to come into your home, do an investigation, file a report with the police department, and maybe take you out of your home and put you in a foster care home. This may not be something you are prepared to do. It takes courage. It takes confidence. As you work through this program, you will gain both. If your circumstances allow, and you feel brave enough, notify the police. If not, do what you are comfortable with and you may gain the strength to do more later.

You can check the Internet to find resources to help you. Do this in a safe environment, such as school or the library. The USA National Domestic Violence hotline number is 1-800-799-7233.

This number is for sexual abuse victims as well as it comes under the umbrella of domestic violence.

Keep on reading as I will bring this subject up frequently. Remember, *you* and your safety are the most important objective in this journey. Only do that which you are comfortable with.

If you don't need this program or one like it, I'm happy for you. I wish no one did. Few people who were sexually violated at a young age are able to go through life without getting help and still be happy. My goal is to help you heal, help you move away from the past, and give you tools to make adjustments so that your life can be everything you want it to be. I have been where you were and my life changed forever because of it.

Marjorie's Story

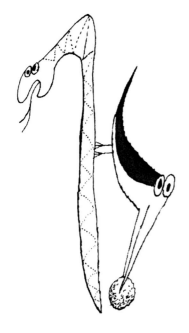

When I was thirteen, my father entered my bedroom, where I slept on the bottom bunk with my rosary under my pillow, and raped me. I screamed repeatedly for my mother, who was a heavy sleeper. By the time she entered my bedroom, my father, holding his robe closed, was standing nearby. She told me I'd had a nightmare. I clung to her with hysteria, begging her to help me, sobbing that it wasn't a nightmare. It did no good. She was convinced I'd had a nightmare and left the room, closing the door firmly. Within days, she found out what my father was doing, had him get me out of bed and come into the living room, where she began interrogating me wanting to know what was happening during my father's middle-of-the-night raids. Terrified that if I described to her what was happening, our happy Catholic family would fall apart, I kept insisting that nothing was happening. I didn't know anyway. I was two years away from finding out how babies were made and at this stage, I thought you bought them at the hospital. That's where we'd bought my baby sister.

My mother told my father to get the belt and then began her litany of "hit her again, hit her again", as he kept hitting me with the belt. We had a framed Declaration of Independence hanging on the wall over our piano. I kept reading the words over and over, "When in the course of human events…" in the hope that I could leave my body. Finally, unable to bear anymore, I screamed, "It's not daddy's fault. It's mine! It's mine!" The beating stopped.

The impact on my family was devastating. My father found a job in a town an hour away and began coming home only on the weekends. Mom covered the windows with Marine Corps blankets and spent all day in bed, sobbing. Where previously mom had fixed all the meals, my four siblings and I began fixing our own breakfast. When we came home from school, there was no dinner waiting. Mom made me her personal servant as she had me bathe her and shave her under-arms and legs. Frightened and sullen at the changes in our life, my siblings and I rarely spoke to each other.

My family life reminded me of a camp of mutilated and injured soldiers from some forgotten war, indescribable in its agony. All the figures were shadowy and disoriented, as if only half-alive and that half living in a well of misery. We moved in and out of our days appearing to wait for some catastrophic event, all of us knowing that once it did, we were ill-prepared to handle it.

At the age of eighteen, after five years of severe sexual, physical, emotional, and mental abuse and one final beating from my father that almost killed me, I stuffed a few belongings into a pillowcase and ran away. Once on my own, I entered what was to become 27 years of unhealthy choices and abusive relationships. I became addicted to sex, had such low self-esteem that I was afraid to have children in case they looked like me, married three abusers, lived part-time in a women's shelter, and wound up twice in a psychiatric ward because of failed suicide attempts. There would be more.

This and much more await those who were sexually abused as a child, if they don't get help before they become an adult. I entered recovery in my mid-forties. My family doctor, who once again asked me whether my father had ever sexually abused me, this time would not take "no" for an answer. He had me see Marcie Taylor, a child sexual abuse specialist in the Los Angeles area, a woman who had been kidnapped at the age of five by two older teenage boys and sexually molested by them at knifepoint. She had also suffered repeated sexual abuse at the hands of her father, who was a Bishop in a Cathedral in Washington DC.

Meeting Marcie, who literally saved my life, was the first step on a long journey, one that took five years to complete. I was married to my third abuser at the time I entered recovery, a man whose abuse was so severe that Marcie said I would never live through it. Trying to go through recovery while you're married to an abuser is like trying to swim upstream with a heavy chain around your neck. In hopes it would help me, I began writing my memoir, titling it *Let Me Hurt You and Don't Cry Out*. It had become the war cry of the perpetrators. I kept writing, knowing that without a happy ending, the book would be pointless.

In the middle of my recovery, my youngest daughter inadvertently commented on what had happened sexually to her two older sisters when they were little. I froze with terror and within minutes, after calling my two older daughters, discovered that they too had been "incested" by my second husband while we were married. Grief and guilt strangled me as my need to become totally healthy accelerated in the hope that it would change the lives of my children. My youngest daughter had been raped at gunpoint by a masked bandit while she worked at a fast food place. That made four out of four in our family to have been sexually abused. Ironically, my only son was a police officer with the Los Angeles Police Department. He had been the Officer of the Year in 1998. I found out that children of an untreated incest victim stand a five-times-greater chance of being sexually abused themselves, for child sexual abuse is a multi-generational illness. At the time I entered recovery, all three of my daughters were married to abusers. By the time I completed recovery, two had rid themselves of their abusers and the third would follow a few years later. As I thought of my grandchildren and their children, a sense of urgency overwhelmed me, compounding my guilt.

I finished working the REPAIR program about the same time that I finished working a Twelve-Step program and was able to rid myself of my abuser. I then went on to do six months of post recovery work. I now had my happy ending.

If you work the REPAIR program vigorously and honestly, you will emerge stronger, happier, safer and with a large number of tools at your reach, tools that will change your life. Parts of this program may be difficult, even painful; parts may be fun and engaging. But you must work the complete program as it is written. Take as long as you need for each step. Some you'll finish immediately; some may take longer.

We use the symbol of the Bridge of Recovery to help you work through this. The Bridge will come up often so that you keep your eyes on the goal and never lose sight of where you are in your recovery and where you are going.

I encourage you to join a Twelve-Step program while you are going through REPAIR. Codependents Anonymous is the easiest one to find. Just call the operator and she'll give you the phone number of the one closest to you. Incest Survivors Anonymous is a bit more difficult to find. There is a list of Resources at the end of this book and includes an 800 number for Twelve-Step Programs.

Use your head, stay positive and one day, you'll be what I am today, "The happiest person I know."

Welcome to the wonderful world of REPAIR!

A Program called R. E. P. A. I. R.

The Stages

- **Recognition:** Recognizing and accepting that your adult problems stem from childhood sexual abuse
- **Entry:** Entering a program of commitment to change your life for the better
- **Process:** Learning tools and techniques that will enable you to become healthy
- **Awareness:** The coming together of reality as you gather the pieces of the broken puzzle your life became, and begin assembling them to see the complete picture. Here you discover the properties of awareness that were God-given promises at birth, but lost at the moment of incest.
- **Insight:** Seeing the complete picture and beginning to return to that which you were prior to being sexually violated
- **Rhythm:** Developing the natural rhythm you had before the incest happened; the blueprint that is the essence of your true nature, becoming who you really are.

Fig. 1-1: Stages of Repair

REPAIR Overview

We are born and we die.
Somewhere between those two major events lie opportunities to be and do all that we want.
It's not a difficult goal—

Unless you were sexually molested as a child.

Webster defines incest as "sexual intercourse between persons too closely related to marry legally". It is a simple, almost clinical description that does not in any way imply trauma or abuse. The all-encompassing and often unspoken reality of child sexual abuse and incest is much broader (both of these words will be used during this program but what is true for one is also true of the other). Anyone in a position of power, who coerces a person of lesser power into any sort of boundary violation dealing with their sexuality, either emotionally, verbally or physically, is a sexual abuse perpetrator. This includes a grandfather who pins his granddaughter down while he fondles her breasts; a father who insists on watching his daughter, against her wishes, while she bathes; an older brother who forces his sister to do oral sex; and any other such boundary violation from the most minor to actual forcible entry and rape. It does not have to be a family member to have the same resultant despair. That despair, whether by a family member or an outsider, can be a life sentence of pain.

This chapter gives you a glimpse of what waits for you if you have been sexually abused as a child or a teenager. It also starts you on your journey of REPAIR.

No one would willingly choose a painful life. But sometimes, early victimization leads you down a path where all you experience is the dark side. Negativity, which has an actual energy field, contains great power and, once it grabs hold, is not easily removed, neither are the wounds that incest causes.

Wounded to their very soul, if not treated, an incest victim either stumbles through a life of despair or dies from it. The tragedy of incest is that, unlike a physical wound, the aftermath can spread to the children, who in turn are either sexually abused or begin a lifetime of unhealthy choices, the direct result of a poor self-image created from shame.

Guilt is the driving force that causes that shame and erodes your self-esteem. The egocentric child perceives all that happens to him as an event they have created and, therefore, are responsible for. A sexually abused child experiences the humiliation and degradation of shame in a monumental way. They either sense the need to keep it secret or are told by their perpetrator that they must remain silent about what is happening, thereby creating more shame. If one could but talk about the pain, incest could be brought into the open and exposed as the real enemy; but humiliation keeps them from speaking the truth. Perpetrators know this, and use that secrecy as a way to protect themselves, and diminish their wrongdoing. They look for the following qualities in their victims: obedience, weak boundaries, innocence and naiveté, as well as someone smaller and easy to manipulate.

Childhood sexual abuse has nothing to do with sex. It is an act of violence with its origins in the need for power and control. Most of the time, the perpetrator was abused himself as a child and is acting out what was perpetrated on him. As an adult, he often becomes the abusive partner in domestic violence and his mate someone who has made victimization a way of life.

As for the sexually abused person often trapped in this cycle, what began as a joyful child becomes a human being who must hide their real self; hence alcohol, drugs, promiscuity, overeating, cutting, and compulsive behavior develop, all designed to create self-loathing. As the years pass, the victim piles shame upon shame with unhealthy choices; their self-image spirals into an all-time low. But you are not the sum total of what you have done. It is necessary during recovery to separate what you have done from who you are, to see that you are not a body with a soul; you are a soul with a body. No matter what has been done to your body, no one can ever touch your soul. It remains pure and innocent. Once you arrive at that realization, you begin to let go of the shame.

Since, after being sexually abused, your self-worth plunges, it is almost impossible to pull out of the negative energy field that has been established and enter one of positive energy. If you add a non-supportive, codependent parent, a society that doesn't want to hear about sexual abuse, and an environment that encourages a lack of boundary setting, the continuing of a life of negativity is almost guaranteed. Also, societal structures such as police procedures, lawyers' tricks, and the media can punish and blame the victim and support the perpetrator.

You all know what it feels like to get out of bed on the wrong side and how it colors your entire day. Incest victims get out of bed on the wrong side every day. They may learn how to hide and deny it, but it's always with them, lurking somewhere in the shadows. "I've learned how to live with it," is a comment I've heard frequently. Why should anyone learn how to live with something as if it were a disease that they could do nothing about, especially when there is an

Fig. 2-1: A Wounded Child

option to heal? Most of the time, child sexual abuse victims are unaware that they have the power to change their own life. Unable to see the light, they become comfortable with the pain.

People with low self-esteem feel they don't deserve the wonderful opportunities available in life. When one presents itself, it is almost as if a master puppeteer pulls their strings and causes them to veer off the path that could have proven a way out of their torment. Most sexual abuse victims move through their days as if that puppeteer were an inescapable part of their lives.

If you can take this negative energy field and, through the use of REPAIR, turn it into a positive one, it will impact the lives of not only your children, but every human you touch. Like the reverse of an epidemic—and incest is at epidemic proportions—the light of REPAIR has the potential to change both the culture of sexual abuse and silence about sexual abuse.

Positive (or healthy) energy repairs and negative (or unhealthy) energy destroys. The negative energy of one person can impact an entire room, and what's worse, an entire day. Destructive emotions increase stress, which lowers the immune system and is thus one of the primary causes of disease.

A wounded child attracts negative people. Somehow, adults who were sexually abused as children, find perpetrators as mates; codependents pair off with alcoholics; bullies find waiting victims; and obedient people wind up with controlling partners. The good news is that once you complete REPAIR, you'll be healthy and your ability to pull in one of a similar nature increases a thousand fold. Doing your small part in a world that doesn't yet see the devastation of childhood sexual abuse has overwhelming rewards.

Despite being a society that is drawn to horror, intrigued with sex scandals, and compelled to watch tragedies on television, we continue to show aversion at the mention of sexual abuse. Like an ostrich burying his head in the sand, we don't want to know about such things. If truth of the sheer number of victims in our society and the far-reaching impact of their trauma was brought to bear on the majority of the population, feelings about a need to take action would change dramatically. Since sexual abuse is so prevalent, we are literally breeding a nation of children with a hole in their soul.

Recovery, in part, is about overcoming that aversion to discussing it. If we can talk openly about the troubles of alcoholism (and today we do), we can talk about incest. Not talking about it is the main reason why incest is epidemic. When wrongdoing is not addressed, it is not dealt with; and when not dealt with, it multiplies. Silence means implied approval and becomes a secrecy that is deadly, for it builds more shame into victims that are already overwhelmed with it.

Fig. 2-2: A Hole in the Soul

Recovery is like a bridge that you need to cross to change your life. In REPAIR the bridge is used as a visualization tool. On one side are the things destroying you. If you turn back, depression, loneliness, despair, suicidal tendencies, addictions, shame-based low self-esteem, and fear of abandonment await you. The list is endless.

On the other side is all the good stuff. There you will find peace, healthy choices, strong self-esteem, a feeling of being centered and stable. There you will find joy. Imagine a life free from pain and emotional instability; a life where waking each morning brings happy anticipation rather than dread; a life where you can stop waiting for someone to rescue you and begin to rescue yourself. All you have to do is keep moving across that bridge. At some point in your recovery, you will learn that, like a carrot on a stick, the other side of the bridge beckons and you will no longer be tempted to turn back.

While the Bridge of Recovery is a visual tool, the REPAIR program is a map to take you across that bridge.

Fig. 2-3: Crossing the Bridge of Recovery

The Rewards for Completing REPAIR

Learning New Truths and New Behaviors

As you move through the program, it is necessary to not only rid yourself of the lies that kept you violated, but to learn new truths and new behaviors. As a childhood sexual abuse victim, you live in a cage of your own construction. But that cage has three sides. The thought of breaking free is not usually a luxury you allow yourself. Freedom has a cloudy picture. It could be scary; it could be devastating. You might have to be responsible for your own actions. You might not be able to blame your sexual abuse anymore when your lives don't go in the direction you wish.

But think about the cage. Is life happy in that cage? Are you experiencing fulfillment? Why are you clutching the bars with a look of terror on your face and your back to the open side?

Setting Healthy Boundaries

In REPAIR, you will learn to not only tear down the behavior that kept you from achieving happiness, but to set healthy boundaries in areas where they are needed. While uncomfortable for a person who was sexually abused, it is a requirement for living a healthy life. Once developed and then put into practice, it will not only alleviate great stress but also bring enormous personal power. Personal power is the one thing a sexually abused person never had, nor did they even realize it was one of their God-given rights. You have learned that responding to upsetting events with anger brings more pain. In reality, anger and the appropriate use of it is one of the strongest motivators to setting a boundary.

A sexual abuse victim displays the lack of personal power in various ways. One of the most prominent, knee-jerk reactions comes from a place of fear and low self-esteem. Instead of thinking through decisions, you immediately make a choice, often not a wise one. Diametrically opposed to this is another behavior pattern of the wounded child. As you grow older, the need for self-protection causes delayed reactions to unpleasant events in your life. Attempting to distance yourself from the pain, you make frantic efforts to keep from feeling its full force. Learning how to set boundaries will not only empower you, it will alleviate both the knee-jerk reactions and the delayed ones.

Fig. 2-4: Inside the Prison of Our Own Making

Regaining Confidence

There are logical steps in the journey from shame to confidence. As you go through the program and learn that the shame is not yours, but in fact belongs to your perpetrator, you relinquish it, little by little. When this happens, you replace it with positive affirmations and other reinforcements of the truth. Through various techniques taught in the Process part of REPAIR, healthy messages and an understanding of what happened bring confidence. People with confidence are not afraid to accept responsibility for their own shortcomings and are able, when criticism comes their way, to recognize the difference between an opinion and truth. These healthy behavior patterns are nonexistent in a victim of childhood sexual abuse. You are too filled with pain to care about learning how to gain confidence.

The shame of what you have become and the behavior you use to hide it grows and is stuffed into closets in your mind. You lean your body against the door and turn a deaf ear to the screams that emit every time you open it to hide another piece of shame. The closets in your mind fill to overflowing and you hit what Twelve Steppers call your "bottom". It is as if your life were on a course of self-destruction, one you have no ability to veer away from as you aim directly for the inevitable, unhappy endings in most areas of your life.

Connecting the Mind and the Heart

At birth, the heart and the mind are connected; but once sexual abuse happens, they separate and the inner self splatters. Like pieces of a broken puzzle, the heart and mind fly to far corners of your inner self where they hide in fear, disconnected from each other and their ability to act as a team. Since you have not developed emotional maturity and the ability to make wise decisions, you do whatever is necessary to fumble your way through life.

During recovery, you will learn to not only connect the mind and the heart, thereby having healthy responses, but locate all the pieces to your unique puzzle, assemble them, and see the picture that emerges—the real you—not the one damaged by sexual abuse.

Developing Emotional Maturity

In normal development, humans pass through stages, each one as important as its predecessor. All stages are needed to create a healthy, responsible, and vibrant human. With the loss of even one, you lose abilities needed to move through life in a healthy manner. As a victim of childhood sexual abuse, you retain only the developmental stages acquired prior to your trauma. You learn to pretend you are an adult, when in truth, children raise other children; children make decisions in the workplace; and, at times, children make choices that directly affect your safety and wellbeing.

It is an amazing experience to come to the beginning of the stage called Process and realize that you are developmentally at the same age as when you were sexually abused. It is even more amazing to feel the emotional growth begin, often in quantum leaps, as you work your way to the end of the program, through post recovery and beyond.

The Return of Our Original Promise of Joy

When you come out of the dark and begin to tell your secrets, the burden lightens. Bits and pieces of light return—the light that was taken from you at the moment of incest. As dark produces more dark, light produces more light and the joy that recovery brings multiplies, even as the despair you suffered in the beginning also multiplied. The old saying *A sorrow shared is a sorrow halved* is true. In talking about your pain, you decrease it. On the other hand, hidden and unresolved sorrow will increase insidiously, and unless you come forward with your own truth, you will remain in a state of despair.

Living Your Life the Way It was Intended

Einstein had an incisive definition of insanity—*doing the same thing over and over again and expecting different results.* The life of a victim of sexual abuse becomes insanity as you continually go down the same road, hoping for a different destination. In this program, using acronyms, the stages of childhood sexual abuse recovery are presented as a different road, one that promises only the happiest of destinations. Requiring rigorous honesty, great courage, and a sincere desire to change your life for the better, it is not for the faint-hearted.

It has been said that it takes all your life to learn how to live. This is a choice, not a mandate. Why not do it sooner? As you move towards the completion of this program, you will make tremendous progress in how to live your life the way it was meant to be.

Each of you is created in the likeness of God and is pure and innocent at birth with a promise of fulfillment. In the case of child sexual abuse and incest, that innocence ruptures. Like a gunshot to the heart, it extracts the joy from life.

The human body has the ability to heal physically, mentally, emotionally, and spiritually. The process of healing in an infected wound often requires lancing. If not done immediately, the infection can spread through the body and perhaps, as in the case of gangrene, cause death. This is, figuratively speaking, what happens to a child who has been sexually molested. Once lanced, a wound will heal, eventually leaving only a faint scar. In REPAIR, you are lancing the wound; but as you do so, you are applying ointment. It is not a difficult process, but it does require courage.

The purpose of this program is to send you into the world with useful tools for recovery. You will not read this book and get healed immediately. It contains exercises as well as thought-provoking questions that will plant seeds. These seeds will turn into blossoms, give you direction and guidance in a world that, at times, will seem dark. Buying this book was a strong step towards simplifying the task of recovery. You must *want* to get well or you wouldn't be reading these words. And the *wanting* is the most important ingredient you will need before you start. The *wanting* will keep you balanced. It will give you purpose and strength. It will become your dearest friend during the times when you are tempted to revert to old habits, the ones that were destroying you and dragging you through a world full of darkness and quiet desperation.

* * *

If ever you doubt whether you are on the right path, think about the children that you know, any tiny child whose eyes you have recently looked into with care and concern. Ask yourself if you can bear what happened to you happening to them. You will then come to realize that making your world safe and happy is a way of making the world safe and happy for your future children and many other children. The despair that fills the world of a person sexually abused touches the lives of everyone who moves within their circle.

Let's talk for a moment about any future children you may have. Although none of you want to believe this could happen to your children, it often does. You are seldom aware that your children adopt behavior patterns you have that lead them into a trap. Qualities such as codependency, obedience, playing the victim role, and weak boundaries are only a few that you will be announcing on an unconscious level to your children. They, in turn, believing that you are all-knowing and all-wise, perceive these behavior patterns as appropriate. Inadvertently they play the same role you did that attracted your original perpetrator.

You think you can protect children by telling them to stay away from strangers. The truth is that most perpetrators are either family members or someone already known to them. You worry about extreme violence and obvious sexual assaults, when subtle kinds of force and manipulation are more likely to happen. You think if you ask them frequently if anyone has touched them in an inappropriate place, you can protect them. That won't do it. Most children will not come forward with the truth. Their shame is too overwhelming. Did you go to your non-abusive parent with the truth when it happened to you? You won't be able to protect your children 24 hours a day, especially as they grow older. What you can do for them is develop new and healthy behavior learned in this program.

They will mimic you and therefore protect themselves. You've already seen what a perpetrator requires as the primary qualities needed in their potential victim. Being strong-minded yourself is no guarantee of protecting your child. You must teach them to be strong-minded. These truths are not meant to frighten you, but to make you aware of the need to become totally healthy as a role model for your future children. Armed with this realization, isn't it time to get busy? It is not only wise but vital that you go through REPAIR before you have children.

You will be so much ahead of what might have been a potentially explosive situation.

Once you complete REPAIR, life will still contain challenges. Frogs will not automatically turn into princes, the lottery numbers won't appear on your pillow in the morning, and you will no doubt eventually have some sort of health disorder at some time in your life. What will happen is that the problems that used to be mountains will change into boulders, the boulders into rocks, and the rocks into pebbles. Objectivity will set in, giving you an inner strength you never had. Instead of bonding with the pain, you will detach and bond with your newly created inner strength.

You will still have good days and bad. Only now you'll have the tools to handle the bad days. You will look ahead, *responding* to the challenges life presents, instead of *reacting*.

Robert Louis Stevenson once said, "The world is so full of a number of things, we all should really be happy as kings." Once you complete REPAIR, you'll look at the world through a different window. It is our hope that by then, you will adopt his words as one of your mottoes.

I invite you to begin the journey that will take you across that bridge and into a whole different life, one you never thought possible. Your journey has six stages. Each one follows the other in a natural sequence as your life and the chaos it has rendered unfold in front of you, waiting to be *REPAIRed*.

Recognition

Knowing we were sexually abused is one thing—

*Recognizing the truth of where the blame lies,
and what we can do about it, is another.*

One of the things you will do in this program is gather evidence. It is necessary to see the complete picture in order to recognize the origins of your unhappy life. No one, and I repeat, *no one*, is born unhappy. It is an acquired deficiency that is a major impediment to the purpose for which you were born—a direct response to all that was done to you and your reactions to those events.

You may or may not regain any memories of being molested. To some, it is a blessing if they don't. What is important is your ability to see the truth. Only armed with the truth will you be able to move through this program and regain that state of mind into which you were born—a state of joy and high expectations of the wonderfulness that life can hand you.

The signs that indicate child sexual abuse as the origin of your problems are like the warning signs of cancer. They illustrate deeper problems. These problems can be mental, emotional, spiritual, and physical.

You become adept at finding ways to either detach from reality or look the other way by creating continuous distractions. Hypervigilance, a condition that causes great and continuous stress, becomes a walking part of you. It interferes with your sleep, your ability to make wise decisions, and most importantly, your capacity for spontaneity and joy. It creates an environment where everyone and everything becomes suspect in the destruction of your own wellbeing. Life, instead of blossoming into the vibrant and abundant promise you expected at birth, is now a desolate affair.

The emptiness of a life filled with the baggage of untreated childhood trauma is one of the saddest things known to man. Sadder yet is the knowledge that you could have been helped. You wait with anticipation for someone to rescue you. No one had rescued you from the abuse, but somehow you think that as your life goes awry, it's only a matter of time before a knight will ride up on his steed and either protect you from life or protect you from yourself. In your naiveté, unable to regain your own power, you fall easy prey to the abusers of the world, thereby prolonging your own agony.

* * *

Having been a teenager who was sexually abused by her father, I can still remember the pain I suffered on a continuous basis during the following years. I avoided mirrors because I thought I was homely. I was moody one minute and, if I heard the latest song by my heartthrob, elated another. My emotions were so close to the surface that it was difficult for me to control them as they skyrocketed all over the place. I developed crushes on male students who were self-assured and good looking and then became embarrassed about it. I had to live with my mother's hatred of me even while I had no understanding of its source. Other students at school made fun of me as my hands shook with continuous tremors. I was thin to emaciation, another reason for the class clowns to use me as the butt of their jokes. This is typical of being in the victim mode. It is as if I had "Kick Me!" written on my forehead—wherever I went, the bullies honed in on me.

As a teenager, your hormones are playing havoc with your body and your head. Nearly one-fifth of the nation's teens are suffering from emotional disorders. Nearly one-half of teens have experienced some traumatic event in their adolescent years. Some 40% have witnessed violence in person. Since teenage years are a time of transition from childhood into adulthood, teenagers struggle with being dependent on their parents while having strong desires to be independent. There is no doubt about it, the teen years are some of the toughest years a child will ever have to go through. It is even tougher for someone who has been or is being sexually abused.

Imagine having an ideal set of parents who are caring and supportive, who encourage you to think for yourself, who are stable and mature—emotionally, mentally, and spiritually—and who exhibit all the qualities required in a loving relationship. A child of such parents would more than likely brim with confidence; his choice of mate as well as of friends would mirror those qualities of his parents; and his chances for making wise choices and planning a successful life would be higher. Unfortunately, this is not the norm. Most people come from varying degrees of childhood trauma. Child sexual abuse is one of the most painful experiences and causes certain behavior patterns—the individual common denominators.

Abuse victims behave and respond in ways that are different from children raised in an emotionally healthy environment. In this book, we will talk about two types of common denominators singular to children of childhood sexual abuse: individual and family systems. Family systems, which we will discuss in a later chapter, show the type of forest you lived in. For now, let's concentrate on the individual ones, the trees.

These common denominators point to the origin of your unhappy life. Once looked at, the picture becomes clearer. It is difficult to believe that a person who had a preponderance of these traits could be living a happy life. Many of them, especially the individual ones, are common to anyone who suffered trauma in their childhood and never healed from the pain. This is a list of identification, not judgment. To help you with an honest appraisal, do the following exercise. Check if any apply to you.

Individual Behavior Patterns	
Behavior	*Y/N*
People-pleasing and rescuing at an early age	
Insomnia	
Excessive need to control	
Obsessive-compulsive behavior patterns	
Needy	
Low self-esteem	
Suicidal	
Weak boundaries	
Unhealthy choices in sexual partners	
Anxiety disorders: panic attackss	
Addictions: drugs, alcohol, sex, food, relationships, etc.	
Eating disorders	
Chronic illness	
Bipolar or Borderline Personality Disorder	
Severe depression	

Let me add a few more of the Individual Behavior Patterns that are more characteristic of teenagers who have been sexually abused:

Cutting or self-injury	
Acting out	
Being bullied	
Running away	
Skipping school / dropping out	

In this chapter you're going to ask yourself tough questions on the above, and then discuss each one. Some of these questions, while painful, are designed to encourage you to take an honest look at where your life is in each area. Get a notebook and begin answering questions in as much detail as possible. As you follow the path of this program, you will discover that you are on a journey of enlightenment. The word literally means to be free from ignorance and misinformation. You received a lot of these in your early years and as you move through REPAIR you will discard all of them. The Buddhist religion considers enlightenment a final blessed state marked by the absence of suffering. This is what you are trying to achieve.

People Pleasing and Rescuing at an Early Age

Have you spent most of your life putting your own needs on hold while you take care of others? How does this feel? Do you resent it? Are you always the one who steps in first to rescue others from their dilemmas? Does adjusting your own behavior so that others will like you better sound like part of what you do? Do you need continual approval and find ways to get it even if it doesn't feel honest or the real you?

If you answered yes to any of these questions, how long have you been that way? Can you remember these traits starting shortly after you were sexually abused?

Insomnia

How often do you get a good night's sleep? Are you using sleeping pills? Do you toss and turn and wake frequently once you do fall asleep? Do you feel exhausted upon waking and tired throughout the day? Do you suffer from nightmares? Are you afraid to sleep and use movies, books, games, online chats to avoid sleeping?

Describe how your world would change if you got all the quality sleep you wanted every night of your life.

Excessive Need to Control

Do you have an obsessive need to control those around you? Do you rant and rave about other people's lifestyles and behavior patterns and lecture them frequently about it? Do you feel that nothing in your universe can work well unless you handle it? Are you forever trying to tell other people how to live their lives? Are you the sort of person that others refer to as bossy?

Answer all of these questions honestly. Take a hard look at how much work it is to run other people's lives. Sometimes doing so is an unconscious choice you make to keep from looking at your own.

Obsessive-Compulsive Behavior

Are you a fanatic about cleanliness and order? Do you have persistent, disturbing preoccupations? Are you opinionated? Judgmental? Does the thought of change terrify you? Are you such a creature of habit that the slightest variation from your routine sends you into nail-biting frenzies?

Make a list of any of the above that describe you. Write next to each item what you'd like to change.

Needy

Do you enjoy your own company? Do you find yourself phoning people frequently, then feeling embarrassed about it? Do you require other people in your life to distract you from sad times? Do you feel as if you pester friends and family with your problems? Do you need to interact with them in order to feel better about yourself? How do you feel about being alone?

Low Self-Esteem

Who do you like best in the world? If the answer isn't "you", you may want to write down why. Do you feel "less than", not worthy, inappropriate, unable to make decisions on your own? Do you make frequent apologies and excuses for why you do what you do? Do you find yourself looking up to almost everyone you know? Do you continually compare your life and yourself with others and feel wanting?

- Make a list of all your character traits that you do not like.
- Make a list of all your character traits that you do like.
- Make a list of all the character traits you would like to have.

Suicidal

Have you ever tried to take your own life? Do you wish you were dead? Do you often feel a sense of hopelessness and despair? Do you feel overwhelmed by your daily responsibilities? Does life seem meaningless and the world a dark and despairing place?

Describe the feelings that accompany these moments and what you think might have caused them, and then write about how it would feel to let them go.

Weak Boundaries

Do you say "yes" when you mean "no"? Do you cringe after reacting without thinking? Do you find yourself spending time with people you don't care for and in situations with which you are uncomfortable? Do you make excuses to avoid certain people and certain choices you have made? Do you think things through before responding? Do you avoid overbearing, controlling people? How comfortable are you with saying NO? Do you have the courage of your own convictions or are you weak-kneed at the thought of defending them?

You have the right to set and hold your own boundaries, those lines you draw that indicate your limits. When a child is sexually molested, their boundary has been violated. Since future abuse was more than likely set up at birth by the type of family systems they were born into, the kind of parents and grandparents they had, and environmental factors, the likelihood of their ability to create and hold boundaries is small. Even if a child had the ability to begin with, once sexually abused, setting its own boundaries becomes a frightening privilege. It requires assertiveness, a quality with which a victim of child sexual abuse has little familiarity; it requires confidence, another quality not common in victims; and it particularly requires a high level of self-esteem that stems from not only knowing what rights they have, but believing they are inherently theirs. Low self-esteem is the core issue in all those who have been sexually abused as children.

Make a list of all activities coming up in the next week, as well as a list of all those people with whom you will be interacting. Then cross out all the things that you don't really want to do and the people you'd rather avoid. What is keeping you from having only the remaining ones on your list?

Unhealthy Choices of Sexual Partners

When you begin dating, you should ask yourself questions about people who you are sexually attracted to. Do they have a problem with alcohol or drugs? Are they physically violent, emotionally unstable, or controlling? Are they honest and fair-minded? What is their personal integrity like? How do they treat their siblings and parents? Do they treat you with respect, consideration and understanding? Do they mean what they say and say what they mean?

These are some of the questions you should ask yourself when you first begin a relationship. If the answers are not right, then neither is your choice. A future with anyone that doesn't rate the right answer to any of these questions is predictable. Don't wait until you are in the depths of despair before you begin to notice the shortcomings of those with whom you have developed an emotional attachment. Since in a wounded child the heart is disconnected from the head, it is no wonder you choose someone who is unstable for your life's mate. People with low self-esteem generally pick partners who do not treat them well or are not of sound and noble character. It is difficult to see that you deserve the best when you do not believe you are the best. Foresight and good judgment, qualities denied to one who has been sexually abused as a child, are essential to your wellbeing. These qualities, among others, will be discussed in a later stage of this program

Make a list of all the attributes you would like to have in a partner. Then, if you are dating someone, ask yourself how many they actually have. This will give you a good indication of whether your life will get better or worse. You will need to be ruthlessly honest and not build excuses. During this program, you will periodically do exercises where you will image the way you'd like your future to be. I cannot emphasize the importance of this enough. Your unconscious is taking notes. Nothing will be wasted. Picture a center in your mind where thousands of volunteers are running around organizing your responses, your thoughts, and your perceptions. Others are busy assembling them into bits and pieces of wisdom that emerge as your inner voices. As you progress through REPAIR, your inner voices will respond to their wake-up call and set in motion a solution for every problem in your life.

Anxiety Disorders

Do you have panic attacks? Do you find yourself having a distorted perception of reality? Are you unnecessarily anxiety prone? Do you have phobias that are unrealistic? Do you bite your nails? Shake with tremors? Have nervous tics or odd behavior patterns with no apparent cause? Are you fearful of situations that most people take in stride? Do you overreact to situations and wish you weren't so sensitive? Do you experience emotional strain, frustration, conflict, psychological stress?

Make a list of any of the above and how you feel about not only having them, but where you think they might stem from, and how you would feel if they were not in your life.

Addictions: Drugs, Alcohol, Sex, Relationships, Gambling, Risk-Taking

Do you use prescription drugs or alcohol to excess? Do you smoke? Are you using any kind of illegal drugs? Do you feel anxiety-prone if you do not have frequent sex with your partner? Do you begin feeling insecure and anxious when not in the presence of whomever you are dating, or in the presence of your friends? Do you modify your behavior and your choices to make whomever you are dating happy even when it is not what you really want? Do you feel you will die without them and/or are nothing without them in your life? When your life is one of despair, obsessing on anything that distracts you from the pain becomes paramount. You develop your own set of rules for survival. Whether they are healthy or not becomes a moot point. The more intense the addiction, whether it be drugs, alcohol, sex, or relationships, the more it takes you away from your pain. You cannot see that you are prolonging it. You can only run for so long before reality settles in.

People who live healthy lives draw on the past for learned and happy memories, and the future to achieve their goals; but they also know how to relish the present moments. Childhood sexual abuse victims don't know how to live in present-time. It is always the despair and pain of the past and wishful thinking for the future. Any present-time awareness needs to be fogged over with an obsession or an addiction, whether it be one with minor consequences—such as obsessive talking—or one of major consequences such as cocaine addiction.

When they drag their baggage behind them, distract themselves with addictions, and live on fleeting hopes of being rescued, is it any wonder that one who was sexually molested sees their life as hopeless and themselves as helpless? For teenagers who were sexually abused, promiscuity often becomes a problem. A sex addiction is the repetitive need for indiscriminate sex with multiple partners.

Fig. 3-1: Dragging Our Baggage Through Life

When you are sexually abused, confusion sets in. You might have enjoyed it. That may set you in a direction of getting more enjoyment once you start dating. As a sexually abused child, you received a subliminal message. That message told you that your main value to another person was through sex. It may cause you, once you start dating, to sleep around. This leads to low self-esteem and often a bad reputation. You don't need that in your life. You've been through enough already. Once you start being promiscuous, it is difficult to stop. Every person you've ever slept with will stay in your head and bring you grief, if not while you're with them, later in life where they poke their heads out at odd moments and bring you shame.

In today's world, teenagers, whether or not they were sexually abused, generally have intercourse with whomever they are dating. Not all use birth control methods. It is better if you don't have sex until you are older, and then with someone you love and who loves you, and especially someone who you want to marry and grow old with. Teenage pregnancies would fill another chapter by itself. Use your head.

If you belong to a church, have a talk with your clergy. If there's a teen group at your church, join it. Promiscuity is a difficult problem to navigate through in life. It brings no rewards. It only piles more shame on top of the shame you're already carrying.

Make a list of any addictions in your life. Remember, an addiction is anything that is a persistent compulsion, an activity meant to distract you from your own pain, characterized by an inability to relinquish it. Describe how you feel about each of these addictions; what you get as a result of continuing to hook into them; and what you achieve if you no longer feel a craving for them.

Eating Disorders

Are you bulimic? Anorexic? Obese? All three of these eating disorders can cost you your life. Do you crave food when you are feeling emotional pain? Do you lie about your eating disorder and sneak food? Do you wear clothes on purpose that hide your bulk? Do you avoid mirrors?

Write a paragraph on any of these that fit you. Describe what it feels like to be bound by any eating disorder you have. How would you feel if they were not in your life?

Chronic Illness

Do you suffer from chronic illness of any kind, either major or minor? How long have you had these? Did the onset of these disorders coincide with your childhood sexual abuse?

As the emotional pain of unresolved conflicts turns inward, it provides a ripe field for physical ailments. A long-term relationship exists between childhood traumas and adult health status. They are linked together by a lifetime web of choices that create chronic illness. Smoking, overeating, alcohol and drug abuse, and unhealthy sexual behaviors are all coping mechanisms sexual abuse victims use to make their way through a minefield of poor choices. As the stress this creates weakens the immune system, it produces cardiovascular problems, chronic obstructive pulmonary disorders, and digestive tract illnesses as well as headaches and muscular and other forms of pain. Even cancer is encouraged by this weakened immune system. The immune system is also suppressed by chronic negative emotion. Remember, destructive emotion is one of the primary causes of disease.

In the life of an untreated victim of child sexual abuse, these potentially life-threatening disorders worsen. One by one, your body systems begin to shut down. Even if you do not physically die, your joy in life dies. Since the human dimensions—spiritual, emotional, mental, and physical—are all inter-related, once the joy is gone, it is only a matter of time before the body follows.

A treated victim, not only has the blessings of being able to pass on to his children the results of his healthy behavior, but his body becomes the primary beneficiary. That victim, who is now a survivor, has a much greater chance to live to a ripe old age. The quality of those years improves dramatically as well..

Bi-Polar Behavior

Do you find yourself ecstatically happy one day and in the depths of despair the next? Do your emotions feel like they are on a roller coaster as you lurch from one mood swing to another? Are you governed by what your feelings are at the moment, rather than working your way through life with logic and sensibility? Do you use your head before you use your words, or do you use your words (and heart) before engaging your mind?

Extremes of emotional highs and lows in the victim, is one of the most prominent repercussions of child sexual abuse. It becomes a way of life that sometimes feels normal. Isn't everybody high sometimes and low at others? No. Healthy people, those who have never experienced childhood trauma, are emotionally stable. It doesn't mean they don't have joy in their life and it certainly doesn't mean sadness never visits them. What it does mean is that these emotions don't reach roller-coaster peaks and valleys as a regular part of their life. On a day-to-day basis, they are emotionally stable, keeping a steady course. Their responses to situations are coherent, reasonable, and rational. They rarely, if ever, have unexplainable highs and then plunges into depression. They are firm in their resolutions and constant in their purpose. If their lives veer off course, they take whatever steps are necessary to restore equilibrium. A sexual abuse victim has little chance of achieving these character traits without recovery.

Severe Depression

Do you feel as if you live on the dark side of life, where happiness is elusive and a sense of peace and tranquility an unreachable goal? Do you feel heavy-hearted and sad, a sense of loss and despair overcoming you on a frequent basis?

Is it difficult for you to enjoy life? Does laughter elude you, and has your sense of play disappeared? Does life seem not worth living?

An overwhelming feeling of hopelessness seems to follow the days of a person who was sexually abused as a child. There may be periodic distractions that bring temporary joy—buying their first car, going on a vacation, going to a party, a new love in their life, and so on—but the overall feeling is one of being unable to cope with whatever may come next to throw them off balance. A sexually abused person doesn't wake in the morning excited about what the day may bring. They only hope it doesn't bring something they can't handle. A constant feeling of impending dread and an almost childlike desire for someone to rescue them colors their day; they're not sure from what, they only know that their burden weighs more than they can carry.

List any of these qualities that describe you. Write about how it feels to have these behavior patterns in your life. Write about what it would feel like to NOT have these behavior patterns in your life.

Cutting and Other Self-Mutilations

Cutting (a form of self-mutilation), which is on the rise among teens, is one of the least understood of the individual behavior patterns of a teenage child sexual abuse victim. An enormous amount of self-loathing lives inside a teenager who has been sexually abused and uses a razor or any sharp object to hurt a part of their body. The complex structure of guilt and shame that child sexual abuse produces has no clear reasoning, and knows only that in their attempt to deal with their pain, hurting themselves in some way brings a temporary surcease. To some, it serves as a distraction from the real villain, child sexual abuse. Much like addictions, such as eating, drinking too much alcohol, doing drugs etc., they take you away from knowing what's happening in your life and the confusion and shame of feeling you are to blame. If emotions are intense, and in your teen years they often are, especially with girls, the desire to cut yourself becomes almost a need. Self-mutilating is dangerous, especially cutting, sometimes leading to serious injury or death. According to CNN, one in five teens says they have purposely injured themselves at some time.

Some of the reasons given for self-mutilation include:
- Not knowing how to deal with stress
- Distracting themselves from their problems and emotional pain
- An unresolved history of abuse
- Low self-esteem
- Feelings of loneliness or fear
- A need to feel in control
- Mental health problems such as depression, anxiety, or obsessive-compulsive disorder

- Wanting to get the attention of people who can help them
- Peer pressure/curiosity

If you are self-mutilating, you start to wear long-sleeved blouses and pants even when the temperature is in the 100s. You think of excuses for how you came to have cuts to ward off any further investigation. Hiding what you are doing becomes paramount.

The self-injury hotline is at 1-800-DONTCUT (1-800-366-8288). If you self-mutilate, please pick up the phone. They are there to help you.

Acting Out

When someone has been sexually abused, hiding it becomes paramount. Your real self, that promise you were given at birth, becomes buried and must be replaced with something or someone else. The need to be or do "something or someone" results in hiding your real self. You are so filled with emotional pain, with fear and anxiety, that taking on an addiction, which we've talked about before, is one way of assuring that your inner self that has been torn apart will not be discovered. You become aggressive, brash, over-confident, or pushy to hide your inner feeling of inadequacy. This is "acting out". Sometimes "acting out" becomes a way of gathering attention, such as throwing a tantrum or behaving promiscuously. That child inside of you, who longs to scream to someone about what is happening, instead must scream in another way. At the age of 13, when asked by a teacher or a parent as to why you are sullen, angry, depressed etc., you can't say, "Oh, that's because my father's been coming into my bedroom at night and raping me."

The Victim of Bullying

When I was fourteen years old, I lived in a small farming community that had square dances at a local farm in the owner's barn. Everyone came to the dance, including me. At that age, I was homely, had crooked teeth, thin hair, was anorexic, and so shy that I rarely spoke without putting my hand in front of my mouth. Due to my father's middle-of-the night raids, my self-esteem was non-existent. The square dance caller would tell everyone to find their partner. I stood in the corner, my heart in my mouth, praying someone would ask me to dance. When no one did, the caller said, "We're not going to start the dance till someone asks little Margie to dance." No one wanted to. Finally, one local yokel spoke up to the buddy standing next to him: "I'll pay you a quarter if you'll dance with her," only to hear the response, "No, I'll pay you fifty cents if you'll dance with her." Large rounds of laughter followed. The bidding went on and on as more teenage boys joined in while I cringed with shame. Finally, someone bid high enough, and I was escorted to the dance floor by the "loser". This happened at every dance, every time I went. The cruelty of this is remembered by the people I went to school with who witnessed it. I never saw it as bullying, assuming I was so ugly I wouldn't want to dance with me either if I were them. But make no mistake; it was bullying.

Bullying is becoming more and more prominent in today's schools, sometimes resulting in the death of a teenager. With new technology and new social organizations, this becomes more of a problem. One cruel person decides to taunt a schoolmate by making fun of her on Facebook. Others follow. If this school-mate has been sexually abused her paper-thin esteem falls to a new-time low. Their ego totally disappears as they slide into a cage from which they cannot escape. Making fun of someone's clothes, demeaning them because of low grades, or bad teeth or body size, are all means to bully another student.

It must be remembered that bullies will only pick on someone whose self-esteem is so low that they can't fight back. It is no fun picking on someone who fights back, so the bully goes on to other territory.

The bully has problems of their own, probably in their home life, that they cannot resolve. Picking on someone weaker is a good way to give themselves a false sense of importance. This is not your problem. This is their problem. Building up your self-esteem as you go through REPAIR and across the Bridge of Recovery will help you with this.

Bullying ends when it no longer hurts rather than when you just cringe and cower. If the response the bully gets is not entertaining, then there is no point in continuing. Having the victim fight back is good fun to them.

Running Away

Each year, two million troubled teens from every social class, race, and religion run away from home. Unhappy in their home life, confused about which choices are right, and vulnerable to peers who want you to think running away is a noble and brave gesture of defiance, they think running away is a wise solution. Disagreements with their parents leave them unhappy and frustrated. In their unstable and highly emotional state of mind, they think, naively, that they will be able to survive outside on their own. But the dangers of runaways and their lifestyles are obvious. Teens on the street are easy targets for rape, prostitution, drug addiction, and violent crimes.

The National Runaway Switchboard, an organization that takes calls and helps kids who have run away or are thinking of running away, can be accessed at www.1800runaway.org. The Nemours Foundation, a non-profit organization in Florida dedicated to improving the health of children, cited the following reasons why teens run away:

- Significant lack of family communication
- Feelings of not belonging or not being good enough
- Physical or sexual abuse
- Fighting or violence between parents

- Problems with parents or blended families (step-parents, step or half-brothers or sisters)
- Problems with non-parental living situation (other relatives, foster care or group home)
- Parental alcohol or drug use
- Loss of parent due to divorce or death
- Parental financial difficulty
- Moving to a new area or school during adolescence
- Friend or peer influence
- Power of gangs

Not all runaways leave home by choice. According to Willie Little, Director of Youth Emergency Services, a non-profit agency that works with the Department of Human Services (Philadelphia), often times teens arrive at the shelter because they have been kicked out of their homes for bad behavior. Teens are also kicked out of their home for being lesbian, gay, bisexual, or transgender, or for not conforming to expected gender roles. Teens in foster care often leave foster homes to stay with friends or other relatives.

Wanting to Leave School

There are many reasons why a teenager might want to leave school: an undiagnosed learning disability, laziness, pregnancy, depression, fear (the massacre at Columbine High sent a message about the powerful ways that bullying can affect a teen's mind), drugs and alcohol, the desire to work full-time and earn money, even if it is only minimum wage.

Teenagers don't think much about the future and their place in it. They live for the moment. While most parents encourage their children to stay in school, some do not give the support and encouragement needed. A teenager may think he/she can earn enough money with their current skills. If they have parents who encourage this, needing additional money in a low-income family, it is no wonder that they drop out. When I was 17 and had just graduated from high school I desperately wanted to go to college. I was told I needed to go to work to help support the family. My parents chose my job and told me I had to turn my paycheck over to them. My response to all the abuse and tight controls was to run away as soon as I turned 18. I was ill-prepared for the real world.

Teenagers who have been abused, either sexually, mentally, or physically, have such low self-esteem that it is difficult to get good grades. Once they begin spiraling down into being a straight "D" student, their desire to improve is very low. Children from a dysfunctional family do not get the help or encouragement they need to get good grades and to see the importance of continuing on in school. Getting a General Education Degree (GED) later is a poor replacement for a good high school education.

All troubled teens have some of the above qualities/problems. When they have too many or they cause distress or despair, they are symptoms of deeper problems, usually stemming from their home life. Sexual abuse is often the culprit. The number of childhood traumas that have their roots in sexual abuse is much larger than people realize. There is nothing quite like shame of your own body and what was done to it to create lives filled with despair and cause you to want to hide that most secret part of yourself.

Taught from childhood that giving till it hurts and turning the other cheek are commendable qualities, you adopt the behavior of codependents to hide your shame. Many of you convince yourselves that codependency is noble. You wind up choosing an abusive significant other, often one who is alcoholic. Do you want that waiting for you once you choose a future partner?

When you choose for your life's mate someone who has already shown signs of contributing nothing but grief, you say you are in love and can't possibly leave. Thinking ahead to the stage when you are no longer in love, but in fact are drowning in reality, is something you never learned and you don't want to learn when you're in that hazy glow that becomes an addiction.

Eating and Body Issues

When your weight creeps beyond what is healthy and heads for obesity, you blame it on Mom's admonishment to eat everything on your plate because the children in China are starving. You buy larger clothes to hide the added weight. You hang around with people who weigh more than you do, so you won't look so bad. You watch a lot of television, so you won't have to think about it. You tell yourself you'll go on a diet tomorrow, or crack jokes about the "see food" diet you're on. You enhance your sense of humor to hide further. Doesn't everybody love a clown? They won't notice your low self-esteem if you keep them laughing.

Perhaps being overweight makes you feel empowered. Surely no one will tangle with you when you are big. When you lose weight because of a diet, you start getting into fear again. It is a false sense of protection. Being big has nothing to do with whether or not you'll be able to protect yourself. You think that if you look unattractive, no one will rape you, another reason for gaining weight.

When promiscuity becomes a way of life at a young age and you sleep with a friend's boyfriend, you tell yourself, with a certain dark humor, that the commandment *Thou shalt not covet thy neighbor's wife*, doesn't mean coveting the husband, only the wife. After all, he's the one committing adultery, not you. Besides, he's not even her husband yet.

Denial goes on and on and you begin setting up behavior patterns that are going to follow you into your future.

Learned Behavior - How We Got this Way

When you see others making healthy choices, walking away from abuse, and taking strong steps to change their lives, you see them as selfish, perhaps even arrogant. When a friend tells you that she is not going to date so and so because he's not good enough for her, you're embarrassed for her large ego. Never mind that he stood her up twice in a row and that his idea of a great date is to show up with his dirty laundry and a bag from McDonalds.

Sometimes, after finding out about your boyfriend's own dysfunctional childhood, you make excuses for them. "How awful that his father hung him from a tree in a gunny sack all day when he was a small boy! No wonder he's always angry." You forget that you too came from a place of dysfunction and yet you never became abusive. Or maybe you did. Childhood pain is never an excuse for molesting or hurting others once you grow up.

A lot of this was programmed as children. What your parents learned, they taught you; what you learn, you pass on to your children. The vicious cycle travels from one generation to another. Like a contagious disease, it impacts every member of the family. A child who was sexually abused is not the only wounded family member. It has been said that witnesses to incest suffer even more than the actual victim. The sister that escaped rape because she lay in an upper bunk grows up, not only feeling guilty for having escaped, but hyper-vigilant and terrified of trusting humans. The brother that can't step in and help feels guilt as does the mother who stands by and watches. The grandparents who see, but don't understand, feel helplessness, which in turn damages their self-esteem. In a wounded family, no one emerges unscathed.

As so eloquently explained in *John Bradshaw on The Family Systems*, each family member has an impact on the other—for good and for bad. The results are so far-reaching that years later that same family gathering for a reunion immediately slips into the unhealthy dynamics originally created in the early family system. The results of child sexual abuse and incest are a downward spiral created through a lifetime of problems and disorders. It takes only one to break the cycle.

For some, hitting what Twelve-Step Programs refer to as their "bottom," may be the only way to recognize that their life is not working. Further signs that occur at this stage are a deepening of despair and flashbacks. Thoughts of death, of throwing yourself in front of a moving truck, chain smoking as you eat foods heavily laden with fat, dressing slovenly and refusing to follow basic good grooming rules, constant negativity, and frequent crying spells followed by periods of despondency, are all part of the pattern of a child sexual abuse victim heading toward his bottom.

If flashbacks happen, they can be terrifying. Where did that picture in your mind come from? A bedroom door half-open has your heart racing with terror and a shadowed picture accelerating in your brain. Why do gray hair and age spots make you suddenly think of your lecherous great-uncle and bring nausea and dizziness? Why does the mention of the book *Lolita* paralyze you with fear? When another in a series of therapists asks if you've ever been molested, why, when your answer is "no", do you feel you just told a lie? Articles in newspapers about incest and sexual abuse of children cause you to begin trembling and head for the bathroom to vomit.

One of the most frequently asked questions in child sexual abuse recovery is remembering, and the role it plays. Some of you remember with searing pictures. Usually those who do, learn to retreat behind a mask of emotional detachment. The ones whose memories lurk in shadowed pictures are generally more overtly troubled, more emotionally unstable, their despairing natures more visible to the outside world. Remembering is not important, but it helps to validate what was.

The lack of remembering does not in any way signify a lack of sexual abuse. If Dad lies in bed in an alcoholic stupor, reeking of whiskey and slurring his words, but you never saw him take a drink and there are no empty bottles nearby, would you say he was drunk? If you came home and Dad was in a raging mood, Mom had a blackened eye and was shaking with tremors every time she looked at him, would you think he might have hit her, especially if he had a history of such a behavior pattern?

So if you remember a nightmare from your childhood where a steamroller was coming over you, if you require large amounts of sex to feel worthy (or can't bear to be touched), if you have been date-raped or if you are dating an abusive boyfriend, why would you not think that you had been violated as a child? If you add to this picture a family history that contains a womanizing grandfather, a sexually promiscuous father, and a codependent mother, all in a patriarchal family, your evidence mounts at an alarming rate.

By now, you should have a clear picture of what a victim of child sexual abuse looks like. You should also know if you fit in that picture. If you are still uncertain or feel that even if it does apply to you, it happened long ago and has no impact on your life today, take a closer look. As we said in the beginning, if you are joyful and in a healthy relationship, working in a positive manner toward achieving what you want, have only positive and uplifting people in your life, and have no screaming child inside of you, filled with trauma and pain, then this program is obviously not what you need. Perhaps curling up with a current bestseller and a bowl of popcorn is more appropriate.

Many victims, sexually abused as children but not by a family member, fail to see that it is as traumatic as incest. In truth, they are one and the same. The definition of the word incest in the dictionary may relate only to blood relatives, but as we clearly described earlier, anyone in a position of power that violates you sexually creates the same world of despair. We are talking about direct and anguishing results of a childhood trauma relating to sex. When it is a family member, especially a parent, the violation of trust and the betrayal by one who you expected to keep you safe can be more deeply ingrained and difficult to work through. That does not negate the pain of being molested by someone other than a family member. Children do not have the mental maturity to differentiate between those non-family members who abuse power for their own purposes and family members who they thought had their wellbeing in mind. The betrayal is the same in both cases and this program can heal the one as well as the other.

Sometimes, behavior patterns that are the result of your incest or other child sexual abuse are the very ones you need to eradicate in order to be happy. They keep you from making an honest appraisal of your life. Twelve-Step programs talk about being "brutally honest". It is a necessary ingredient in working this program. Listening to destructive messages from your childhood rather than arriving at your own conclusions; clinging to old ways because they are familiar—no matter how painful—instead of accepting change; and lacking faith in your own ability can all keep you from RECOGNIZING what your life has become and hold you back from taking the first step onto the bridge.

Recognizing the Duplication of Relationships

Victims of childhood sexual abuse often re-enact a script from their growing-up years, hoping this time it will turn out differently. As they get older, they find themselves drawn to people who have similar qualities to their perpetrators. This is almost always done on an unconscious level.

The reasons are complex. You had a love/hate relationship with the perpetrator and when you never achieved a healthy bonding with them as children, that need went unsatisfied. Once you start dating, you look for satisfaction in the face of every potential partner. Many a victim of sexual abuse grew up saying they would never marry anyone like their father, and yet they continued to do so over and over.

You needed someone who could fill the empty hole inside yourself and as adults find, sometimes in almost exact replication, the dual nature of your original family. On the outside, charming, bright, enlightened... on the inside... seething sexual abuse and manipulative, controlling qualities.

Most of the time, people in a position of power appear all-knowing, and all-powerful, therefore worthy of being someone with whom you wish to spend the rest of your life. The truth is that your unconscious mind, because of low self-esteem, feels unworthy of a partner who is healthy, so you place the dysfunctional one you chose on a pedestal, thereby blocking their true nature and re-creating your own misery as a wounded child.

Recovery can become the ointment you place on your wounds. Without the right program, the ointment may not help. When floundering through recovery without proper direction, you run the risk of prolonging the time by joining unhealthy groups, choosing a therapist who knows nothing about recovery from child sexual abuse, or getting sidetracked by reading books that have little to do with healing from the abuse.

Let's get you started on that first step across the bridge. Now that you have recognized the origin of your problems, you are ready for the second stage of REPAIR.

Entry

New beginnings are always difficult,
But they are the only means
To moving forward with your life.

For without change, we die, locked in the same prison.

A pattern seems to precede entry into recovery during your teen years. After being molested, as you grow older, your life starts to fall apart, a process so gradual that you may not be aware of it. One failed relationship leads to another. What started out as partying becomes alcoholism; having a crush on another student somehow leads to promiscuity and you wonder how did you get there? The lack of confidence that you thought was the result of being young, remains. Making wise choices eludes you and you begin to realize that your young life presents little joy; that some of your choices add to your spiraling self-esteem.

You're not sure who or what to blame. You thought life would get better as you got older. If only this or that would happen, all would be well. But it never does and you never get well. Your despair deepens and hope dies. Bad experiences based on unhealthy choices pile up in closets in your mind with doors you won't open. You are hardly aware that those closets contain childhood trauma from your sexual abuse and that you have been trained early on to keep them under lock and key.

Cynicism, low-grade depression, and anger begin. It's so insidious that you scarcely notice. Then one day, you wake up and realize life is going too fast and it's not turning out the way you wanted. You run out of places and ways to hide. The closets in your mind fill to capacity and can no longer hold back the dam. You are ripe for entry into recovery.

You have reached your "bottom". The term "bottom" has been mentioned previously in this manuscript. It is an interesting term, coined by Twelve-Steppers and literally means the lowest point. You don't reach this overnight.

Having a high tolerance for pain can keep you out of recovery. That very tolerance is why you remain in relationships that don't work. During the passage of time, you heap trauma upon trauma, incorporating more unhealthy behavior patterns into your life, and losing precious time that could have been joyous. From childhood on, like one playing a game of limbo stick, instead of walking away, you continuously readjusted. No wonder the abuse grew as your tolerance increased.

While going through REPAIR, you will discover, as you learn to set boundaries, that your tolerance for pain will decrease. Abuse aimed in your direction that you used to grit your teeth over will no longer be acceptable. You will start seeing with great clarity not only who the good guys and the bad guys are, but what appropriate behavior is and what isn't. Once completing REPAIR, you will get used to people asking why you've become so intolerant. Those voices will be the ones of others who have not yet learned to set realistic levels of tolerance. It is one thing to be patient in a grocery line, and quite another to put up with a vicious verbal attack from a fellow classmate, enabling them to continue their bad behavior.

A frequently asked question is why do some who suffer the most severe of traumas deal well with the repercussions and others who seemed to have minimal abuse grow up with more painful adult years. The degree of what happened to you is not always proportionate to the degree of your fate. Many factors play a part. A child who had a loving and supportive mother may find it easier to overcome the incest damage from her father. Another, whose incest trauma was relatively minor but also had an abusive mother and other heinous environmental factors, may find herself a drug addict and prostitute at an early age. The total picture needs to be seen. But in all pictures, sexual abuse and its resultant shame are still the core issues.

Sometimes it is easier for you to look at a much milder trauma as the focal point for why your life is scarred. Remembering the pain of not getting a hoped-for bicycle at Christmas or a cruel taunt of a schoolmate is much easier to deal with than the real reason you are suffering. Opening the closet that contains a sexual abuse perpetrator and the slaughter of your own innocence is not something you are so willing to look at. Many of you approach recovery in stages. As you gradually work up to the real culprit, you gain courage. Do not despair if you open only the less traumatic closets first. In time, every closet will be opened.

Entering recovery occurs in various ways. The most prominent are:

Individual Therapy

This sometimes begins at the urging of a family physician, a spiritual advisor, or a family member who can no longer bear to watch the individual suffer. If you are in a position to have a therapist (either because of a supportive parent or because your school provides one), if possible, shop for a therapist as you would for any major purchase; ask questions, request references etc. Not all therapists are created equal. Check their credentials; interview them. Have they ever worked with a patient on childhood sexual abuse issues? Have they themselves or any family member ever experienced incest? How long have they been practicing? What is their success rate in bringing clients through recovery? Do they have additional tools to suggest to help you on your journey? Brainstorm other questions, so you will be prepared when you go to your first appointment.

Some therapists are not qualified to deal with such a sensitive and painful issue as incest. While a guided tour is optimum, it is always possible to find your way along the bridge without a guide. You are never really alone. Additional help is available. If that help is chosen carefully and utilized to its fullest, you can complete the program without a therapist. It is important that I reiterate, having the right therapist, one who either has child sexual abuse in her background or who has worked extensively with that problem, is a vital part of recovery. On the other hand, having one who has no experience can only hinder or damage your journey through recovery.

Group Therapy and Programs

Twelve-Step Programs, e.g. Codependents Anonymous, Incest Survivors Anonymous, Adult Children of Alcoholics, Alcoholics Anonymous, and others, as well as recovery groups in local churches, sexual assault centers, domestic violence groups, etc., all prove to be not only invaluable help but almost a necessity in finding your way across the bridge. Even teenagers are welcome in Twelve-Step programs. If they shop around, they can find meetings that have members in their age group. All Twelve-Step groups can be accessed by a simple phone call to an operator who has numbers for all available groups. We will discuss group therapy in greater length during the PROCESS part of this program. They provide the maps you will need to complete your journey. Sometimes, working hand in hand with more than one is a good idea. Here, common sense enters the picture. Check The Lamplighter Movement at **www.thelamplighters.org** to see if there is a chapter in your area. If not, check their "Start A Group" page and download the Lamplighter Facilitator Guide to see if you would like to start a group yourself. It is so easy and would empower you in many ways. Empowerment is what you need.

If you join a group that is non-supportive of your goals, is not all-embracing of your problems, and does not use personal integrity as their guideline, they are not right for you. If they prove interesting, but of little help, continue your search for another group, one that will help you to move across that bridge.

This includes Twelve-Step Programs as well as others. Just because you are uncomfortable with one Twelve-Step group doesn't mean it is the fault of the group. Perhaps the participants are not quite tailored to the kind of support you need. Being in a group that has members of your age group would probably be more comfortable. Just as all therapists are not alike, not all groups are alike. Unfortunately, some recovery groups have adopted destructive behavior with excessive control and power plays. They can sabotage progress and prey on a victim's vulnerability. It is up to you to pay attention to your inner voices—that intuitive part of you. It will never lie. If you feel that a group is not right, it probably isn't. But don't make a snap judgment. As with Twelve-Step programs, give each group six sessions. If you still feel uncomfortable, it is time to search for another. Every time you expose yourself to other people's dysfunctions, you run the risk of creating more of your own. You don't need something like that to slow your progress in getting healthy.

Check the Internet for groups that you can join online. A significant amount of help is available. Just make sure that the group you join is a legitimate one for recovery. The Internet, while a useful tool, also has groups that are not for recovery but instead are unhealthy groups.

For those not familiar with the Twelve-Steps, they are listed both here and in the Resource section at the back of this book.

1. We admitted we were powerless over others and that our lives had become unmanageable.

2. Came to believe that a power greater than ourselves could restore us to sanity.

3. Made a decision to turn our lives over to the care of God as we understood God.

4. Made a fearless and searching moral inventory of ourselves.

5. Admitted to God, to ourselves, and to another human being the exact nature of our wrongs.

6. Were entirely ready to have God remove all these defects of character.

7. Humbly asked God to remove our shortcomings.

8. Made a list of people we had harmed and became willing to make amends to them all.

9. Made direct amends wherever possible, except when to do so would harm themselves or others.

10. Continued to take personal inventory and when we were wrong, promptly admitted it.

11. Sought through prayer and meditation to improve our conscious contact with God, praying only for knowledge of His will and the power to carry it out.

12. Having had a spiritual awakening as a result of these steps, we tried to carry this message to others and to practice these principles in all our affairs.

A Combination of Both

When you utilize the services of both, the qualified therapist will be your primary guide and the Twelve-Steps and other programs part of the path you take. There will be times when a one-on-one and cross-talk—a style not followed in most Twelve-Step programs—is what you need at the moment. People in programs, while they too are on a journey of healing, do not necessarily have the expertise that a therapist can provide. For those sensitive moments when you require privacy and wisdom that may not be available from the lay person, a trained therapist is your best bet. If your parents have medical insurance, that may be covered, but there again, especially if your perpetrator is a member of your nuclear family, you will need the help of a supportive parent. Often there are hidden benefits that cover post-traumatic stress.

Supportive and Non-Supportive Family Members and Friends

I need to say a word here about talking to your parent or caregivers about what you are going through. This is a difficult matter to pick through wisely. If your perpetrator is one of your parents, it may not be wise to discuss it with the other parent. If the abuse is ongoing, it is important that you get help. Do you have a grandparent who is supportive and wise to intercede for you? Is there a counselor at school that can help you with this? You don't want to make matters worse by telling a mother who refuses to believe you and then tells your perpetrator, whether it be a sibling, the other parent, or an uncle or grandfather. What the perpetrator is doing is against the law, even if that person is a member of your family. You have the right to call the police, check with a trusted clergy, or call Child Protective Services.

One of the most important needs you will have is the circle of friends and family who make up your support group. Not everyone will be on this list. Your nuclear family may not want to dredge up old family stuff. Worse yet, they may not believe you and may ridicule your efforts. Anyone who does not take your recovery seriously has no place in your inner circle. Mom may not want to desecrate Dad's image. In patriarchal families, keeping Dad on his pedestal is mandatory. Secrecy is the biggest reason child sexual abuse is epidemic. Why would you want to protect someone who has physically violated you? Why would you want to choose someone who encourages you to protect that person as part of your support group?

Eliminate those who might hinder your progress. Emphasize that you are on a journey and that arriving at the end is the only thing that matters. Keep only supportive people in your life. Any attempts to sabotage your recovery will keep you from reaching the end of that bridge.

Seek those willing to listen—those who genuinely care and encourage you. You will be surprised how many who touch your life will soon be touched by yours. Often, during recovery, you meet kindred spirits who, if it were not for your courageous efforts in coming out of hiding, would not be able to face their own childhood traumas. The sad truth is that more people have been traumatized by sexual abuse, either to themselves or a loved one, than have not.

As we have already learned, the trauma of a victim of child sexual abuse has an impact on all family members. In looking forward to your future with a mate, remember that two healthy people have a great chance of finding happiness in a relationship. One healthy and one not-so-healthy have a more difficult chance, and two unhealthy people stand very little chance of having a happy life together. This should give you an incentive to go through recovery. If you are currently dating someone who has childhood trauma problems themselves that need to be addressed, don't lose site of the fact that your primary purpose is getting yourself healthy, not your partner. If something beyond that happens, such as your partner getting into recovery, it will be an added blessing.

It is vital that you begin recovery before you get to the marriage and family stage of your life. Having gone through the REPAIR program, you will no longer be attracted to abusive people. Only healthy people will be drawn into your circle.

As you cross that bridge, you will begin to see your boyfriend/girlfriend—if they are an abuser—in a different light. Power plays, manipulations, and controls will be more obvious and you will be less willing to buy into them. As you begin to set boundaries, they may retaliate by accelerating their own unhealthy behavior. This is no time for a faint heart. If separation from an abuser gives you the courage to work through your own recovery without faltering, this may well be the path you have to follow.

If friends or family harass you to split up from an abuser before you are ready, your despair will deepen. You never walk alone until your legs are strong enough to hold you. Let those who care know what you are going through, and that all changes have to be done in your time frame, not theirs. When you are ready, although it may still be painful to go through a separation, you will have the strength to walk through it. If your loved ones choose to abandon you because they can't bear your pain, that is their decision. If the bond is strong enough, this will not happen. And if it does, they may return when you have completed recovery.

Codependents are hampered in their progress by focusing on the needs of their significant other rather than their own. It is extremely difficult to pull away from this trait. As you build strength by working through REPAIR, in time, it will be easier. While crossing this bridge, it is imperative that you put your progress in the program above all other needs. If your significant other, abusive or not, cannot be supportive of this, you may eventually decide to go it alone.

A word here about those fortunate enough to have a supportive significant other. It can be hard on them to help you work through recovery. They may be confused. As you begin going through the recovery process, some things will be difficult for them to understand. Certain facets to your relationship may be put on hold. This adds to your mate's confusion. Using clear communication to keep them posted on your progress will enable them to be supportive of your journey. They may not always understand what you are going through, but letting them know it will improve not only your own life, but the relationship the two of you are building will go a long way toward enlisting their support. Twelve-Step

Programs are available to them as well. Encourage them to attend. Working a Twelve-Step program is always an improvement in anyone's life.

It is not a good idea to attend Twelve-Step meetings together. This can serve to inhibit both of you as well as create enormous conflicts once you leave the meeting. Many a couple has gone their separate ways because one or the other was dismayed at their partner's revelations at a meeting regarding disputes in their private lives. If you go to a meeting alone, while there, you may arrive at the appropriate way to approach your mate on an issue that has long been churning, but blurting it out while he or she is sitting next to you is an almost guaranteed way to sabotage accomplishment. The Twelve-Steps were founded on anonymity and as such, all participants are bound by their word to not repeat anything they hear. This makes it a safe place. Twelve-Steppers, new to the program, are fragile and it is taking all the courage they have to keep going in recovery. They don't need more conflict in their personal life.

* * *

Our point of entry may occur when you reach your bottom. Everyone's is different. It may be a drunk driving charge, finding out you have just tested HIV positive after being promiscuous, winding up in the Emergency Room from a failed suicide attempt, a parent or sibling saying they can no longer bear being around you, or the timely realization of your own acute misery. Sadly, the bottom for some is death.

Sometimes, no one urges us. A word or phrase heard on a talk show, a movie or TV program that bears an eerie resemblance to your own life, can be the spur that sends you into a program. In the beginning, even the word *recovery* is foreign, as if it belongs to someone you've read about in a magazine but has no bearing as an answer to your own tormented life. Whatever it may be, keep following whatever thread leads you onto that first step.

Commitment

There is little purpose in entering recovery without commitment. Many child sexual abuse victims, having heard it is the answer to their prayers, race off to a local Codependent Meeting. They wander out two hours later, scratching their head. *Who wants to listen to other people's problems? I'm trying to get away from them,* or *everyone in there looked like a loser. My life isn't that bad.* Sound familiar?

Rather than focusing on what you see, listen to what you hear at the meeting. You may see a room full of troubled people, but what you are hearing is a room full of courage. The saying in Twelve-Step programs that you must attend at least six meetings has a lot of validity. Something magical happens by then. You start to get it. The feeling that you are in the right place overwhelms you as you begin to identify with their stories. Only a sense of commitment will carry you through those meetings. Anyone who survived years of living with abuse, can certainly survive six meetings at Twelve-Steps. In time, you'll wonder how you ever got along without them.

Only one person can turn your life around—*you*. No one can travel the journey for you. Friends may be supportive of your efforts. They may applaud your progress. But in the dark of night, in the middle of that bridge, when you look down at the deep waters and want to turn back, your sense of commitment will keep you moving forward. You must find a secret place inside of you to bond with and make a pact with. You must promise not to falter or run.

If you knew for certain that going across that bridge would change your life dramatically to a place where life became everything you wanted, would you turn back? Of course you wouldn't. While there will be times during your journey when recovery may be painful, times when the load seems too heavy to bear, you must separate yourself from those fears. Nothing could be as bad as what's behind you. Lean into the wind and feel the presence of something happening in your life greater than anything you could have predicted. You are in the process of becoming all you were meant to be. That is an awesome promise.

Everyone's timetable for crossing that bridge is different. Many factors come into play. Only you will know when it is time to enter the next step in your program. Only you will know when it is time to confront your abusers or even the manner in which to do so. Recovery is very individual. One person may take five years; their reasons don't define you. If another has already arrived at the end of the bridge and you are still floundering at the beginning, don't give up. Often, quantum leaps occur at unexpected moments that will propel you forward at a speed you couldn't have predicted.

Everything you are learning takes time to process. Parts of it will feel comfortable, even exciting. Interviewing cooperative family members to construct your history cannot only prove enlightening, but entertaining. Other tasks may not feel as comfortable. While you move across that bridge, you will be building strengths that, in the beginning, you could not have predicted. As in building a house, the foundation will be strong enough so that when you get ready to place the roof, it will seem like an easy task.

Preparing for Your Journey

As with all journeys, before you begin to cross that bridge, one must prepare. Your preparations should include plenty of sleep, quiet time alone for daily meditation, and a healthy diet that follows the basic food groups, especially plenty of fresh fruits and vegetables. Eating well means feeling well. If you don't believe this, spend one week eating only junk food and the next eating healthy food. You are in a healing mode, not only emotionally, mentally and spiritually, but physically.

Keep your fluid intake high, drinking at least eight glasses of water a day. Surround yourself with pleasant and healthy activities, and set aside a part of each day for exercise. One of the best is walking. If you have a park or a scenic setting nearby, combine a daily walk with meditation. Having that physical side of you in a good place will go a long way toward promoting total wellness and will do wonders for your emotional stability.

Check with your local health food store. A number of herbs have a calming effect. Chamomile and other herb teas aid sleep disorders. Evening Primrose Oil, available at any drug store, is a great natural way to promote emotional stability. Avoid cigarettes, alcohol, and excessive sweets. Alcohol is a depressant, and a 30-minute walk will do you more good than any alcohol. Follow these rules for good sleep:

- Keep caffeine intake to a minimum.
- Use salt sparingly, if at all.
- A hot bath with a good book, soft music, and a lighted candle (white for serenity) has a calming effect before bedtime.
- Eat early in the evening and avoid large meals, if possible.
- Always retire at the same time.
- Establish a comforting and stabilizing ritual prior to bedtime, i.e., lay out clothes for the next day, brush your teeth and bathe, set the clock, read something bland for a few minutes before turning the light out.
- Avoid intense or worrisome phone calls before retiring, as well as any late-night dealings that may encourage stress.
- Don't exercise to excess in the evening—a short walk perhaps to ease any tension. Daily exercise has the added benefit of improving sleep.
- Make sure the room temperature is comfortable.
- If you begin to toss and turn, get out of bed and fix a glass of warm milk or non-caffeine herbal tea. Insomnia intensifies once you begin worrying about it; so anything you can do to distract yourself eliminates the problem.

Fig. 4-1: Rules for Good Sleep

Maintaining these simple rules will ease the discomfort of your journey. While the symbolic bridge you're on may sway, and the waters below may look dark and scary, you need only utilize the suggestions in this program to find the courage to keep going. One additional source of help for anxiety is the following:

http://anxietyanddepression-help.com/firstaid.html

As I said earlier, new beginnings are always hard. We prefer the predictable, the timeworn regime. Your life may be miserable, but it's yours and it's familiar. Following the program, REPAIR, will require change and change is difficult. But change is what brought your life into a place of darkness, and change will serve as the tool to take you into the light. No one escapes change, a constant in life. So, since it is inevitable that you must face it, wouldn't you prefer that which will bring good? Keep these truths in mind as you approach the next stage of our program.

In the coming pages, you will find many exercises that, at first, may seem overwhelming. Do all of them in your own time. None are designed to be done overnight. They may require much thought and the proper moment to approach them. Or perhaps you'll want to do them more than once. There are no rules except to follow the stages. Put this book aside and work on another part of the program, perhaps attending Twelve-Step meetings, if you are not yet comfortable with them. They are all tools to encourage you to begin thinking about the stages you will be going through. Words have power, and the more words you write in these exercises at the moments when they are called upon to put in an appearance, the stronger you'll feel.

We can promise that if you follow through on a pact to stay on the bridge, the rewards will be overwhelming. As you come closer to the end of that bridge, wonderful things waiting on the other side will become visible. You'll develop a sense of wellbeing. You may find yourself singing and smiling more, as if you know something others don't. You do. Plans will begin to formulate in your head about what to do with the rest of your life. It will all be hazy at first; but little by little, everything will become clear. Keep this in mind as you progress to the next phase of REPAIR.

Process

Do what works—

And everything else will fall in line.

I mentioned earlier building a house. When you do so, you start with the basement or a foundation. From there the walls take shape, giving you a frame. Soon the roof falls in place and windows and doors follow. If you want the house to last for many years, the right tools and quality materials are needed to build it. Shoddy workmanship, cheap materials, inaccurate building instructions, and especially a poor choice for a site, all these will cause your dream home to become a nightmare as it falls apart. This should come as no surprise.

In many ways, the life of an incest/child sexual abuse victim is much like a house that was poorly built. Parents that are ill-equipped themselves, can hardly raise healthy, vibrant children. Unhealthy messages from those who are in charge of creating your personality, your temperament, and your way of making choices are inevitable. Victims of child sexual abuse need to rebuild their **own** home.

The right tools are important. They will include the following:

Media on Recovery

The marketplace is overflowing with media on recovery: books, including electronic books, the Internet, CDs, even smart phone apps. Check out blogs written by people who have also been sexually abused. Social media groups such as Twitter, Facebook, MySpace or Tumblr have groups that share information on how they are doing. First-hand knowledge often gives a different perspective to the professional word. Every conceivable mental and emotional aberration known to man has been researched and written about. Child sexual abuse is no exception. Do a Google search. You'll be surprised what's out there. Choose from those that provide insight and support for your particular need. This will give you additional knowledge and deepen your understanding of what happens to a molested person and why. You are embarking on a journey, one of education as well as of healing. No education is complete without accessing the wide variety of tools that are available in today's world.

A book downloaded on your iPhone, iPod or iPad is especially an invaluable tool for getting well. There are a number of ways to listen to your electronic device: while you are driving, while you clean the house or do yard work, on your morning hike, listening while you soak in a hot bubble bath. These words will become a part of your vocabulary and will change your way of thinking, so it is important that you recognize them as truth. The key is not only listening, but hearing. Reinforcement comes through repetition. That's why it is so important to listen frequently to those that are pertinent to healing from child sexual abuse. John Bradshaw's *Healing The Shame That Binds You* is one of the most beneficial and is available in CDs, paperback and electronic books. At the back of this book is a resource guide with media suggestions for recovery and post recovery.

If you are using a "family" computer, be aware that someone may be checking your surfing history so you might need to take steps to cover the tracks of your "browsing history". Fortunately, this is a matter of a few clicks depending on which browser you use.

See http://www.computerhope.com/issues/ch000510.htm

The Bridge

The Bridge, a visualization tool, is a vital part of REPAIR. Look at the illustration in Chapter Two frequently and use it as a source for imagery. If you were going to be taking a trip to Europe, you would no doubt think often of the wonderful sights you were going to see. You would count the days until you experienced the pleasure. You wouldn't be worrying about how much the trip will cost, for fear that you would change your mind. You would only think about the importance of your destination. The Bridge represents the journey you will be taking and what lies on the other side represents your destination. What lies on this side is what will continue to happen in your life if you don't begin. The most important part of a journey is the first step. After that, you need only keep on moving.

Do the following exercises before you enter this Bridge. (As with all the exercises in this book, if you are more comfortable with it and need the extra room, write your answers in your own journal or notebook.)

What Waits Behind Me If I Don't Enter the Bridge?

(Examples: shame, alcoholism, promiscuity, eating disorders, suicide, despair, health problems, cutting/self-mutilation, unhappiness, poor choices, codependent behavior patterns, acting out, running away, wanting to leave school, the victim of bullying etc.)

In the space provided below, describe vividly each of these that are prevalent in your life as well as any others you can think of.

_____

_____

_____

_____

_____

_____

_____

_____

_____

_____

_____

Fears You Will Encounter as You Cross the Bridge & Solutions to Combat Them

(Examples: Problem—I'll feel too alone. Solution—I'll build a strong support group among friends, family, and groups and utilize them whenever I feel this way. Problem—Looking at the pain of what happened is too overwhelming. Better the devil I know than the devil I don't. Solution—I'll check my list of all the things waiting for me at the end of the bridge, then compare it to the list behind me. My choice will be easier after that.)

Write your own list and possible solutions

Problem	Solution

Keep in mind that inside each of us lies an untapped well of strength. We must be strong enough to cross the bridge; we have already survived so much.

What Lies on the Other Side of the Bridge, Waiting for Me?

Examples: joy, strong self-esteem, healthy choices, honesty, peace, a feeling of being centered and capable, fulfillment, problem resolution, serenity, etc.

As you write, picture each of these to their fullest. They will act as a beacon guiding you across the bridge and one day will be a part of your life.

Now, picture yourself entering the bridge. Like all journeys, you want this one to be successful. It is the most important one you will ever take. Crossing this bridge will bring you to a world beyond your wildest expectations. Reread the lists you have just written at least once a day to reinforce the purpose of your journey.

_____

_____

_____

_____

_____

_____

_____

_____

_____

Construct a Magic Mirror

This may be the most significant thing you do as you cross that bridge. Your Magic Mirror will become your new parents. When you were a child, inevitably you received a lot of messages, some of which were unhealthy. *Don't touch yourself there. Bad girl. You're always lying about everything. I knew you were going to turn out like your father—no good. I'll tell you what you like and don't like. You're lazy.* And so on. Unfortunately, there were probably more negative messages than positive. Your brain is stuffed with them and what's worse is you no doubt believe them. It takes tremendous force for an adult to withstand these "not okay" messages, much less someone in their teens.

You will need to get rid of every one. But it is not enough to rid yourself of these damaging messages. Replace them with healthy ones. Make a list of all the unhealthy messages you can remember, no matter how small or how early they were given. Even if the one giving the message convinced you they were true—but you know differently—write them down. Read over the list of unhealthy messages you received as a child and rewrite them the way you would like. Below is an example of what your list might look like.

Unhealthy message	Healthy replacement message
You never do anything I tell you.	I choose to do what I think is right.
You're stupid. You can't even get an A in English.	I'm very bright and can get an A in anything I choose.
Your room is a pigsty. It shows what your mind is like.	I'm a creative person and that's what happens when your mind is full of creative ideas.

Now, write some of your own.

Unhealthy message	Healthy replacement message

Fig. 5-1: The Magic Mirror Gives You the Power to Create Your Life

Next, you will need to gather affirmations for your Magic Mirror. Select any from the lists below that resonate with you. If you feel a strong emotional reaction to the affirmation, that is an indication you might have an issue around that. The following are some suggestions.

Healing

- No wound heals overnight, but little by little.

- As my heart heals, I will learn to love in exciting, powerful new ways.

- My maturity level will grow in proportion to the amount of pain I put behind me, and the wisdom I acquire as I move through the stages of REPAIR.

Courage

- The only antidote for fear is courage.

- I will trust that all is well, in spite of any fears I have.

- An unknown fear is better than a familiar pain.

- Whatever I fear grows in proportion to my obsession with it.

- I can get through dark situations. I only need to go as far as I can see. By the time I get there, I'll be able to see further.

- We all have monsters. Maybe it's fear of new situations. Maybe it's jealousy. The more attention I give the monsters, the more powerful they become.

Overcoming Problems

- A mistake is something I do; it's not who I am.

- There is no problem too difficult to handle with all the help available to me.

- All the problems are in my head. So are the solutions.

- Unfinished business doesn't go away.

- The only thing that's really the end of the world is the end of the world.

Anger

- I have a right to feel anger, and a responsibility to deal appropriately with my anger.

- I may need to get angry to set a limit, but I don't need to stay angry to enforce it.

Pain

- Recovery does not mean freedom from pain. Recovery means learning to take care of myself when I'm in pain.

- I can stop my pain and get control of my life.

- Pain is inevitable; suffering is optional. - Kathleen Casey

- I will accept pain and disappointment as part of life.

- If sorrow or pain enters my life, I can lean into it and become stronger.

Change

- I'm the only one who can change my life.

- The more choices I make, the more alive I feel. The more alive I feel, the healthier my choices.

- I am capable of making my most important decisions.

- Losing my freedom of choice is a bitter pill to swallow.

- There is no way to avoid changes in life, so why not make them positive ones?

- I will give up regrets about the past and fears about the future. I will make the most of this day.

- Healthy choices are all around. I can learn to make them.

Attitude

- "As we think, so we are." My mind works powerfully for my good, and just as powerfully to my detriment when I allow fear to intrude on my thoughts.

- A change of attitude is all I need to move from where I am to a better place.

- I need to believe that I deserve the best life has to offer. If I don't believe that, I need to change what I believe.

- If I always do what I've always done, I'll always get what I've always had.

Negativity

- I will avoid negative people.

- I can learn to let go of negative energy.

- If someone else has a bad day, it doesn't necessarily have anything to do with me.

- I don't have to believe lies.

Relationships

- I can recognize the difference between relationships that work and those that don't.

- Boundaries are worth every bit of time and energy it takes to set and enforce them. They will provide me with more time and energy.

- Friends are a joy. Today, I will reach out to my friends.

- If I think I'm the one who's finally going to change someone, I may be the one who gets victimized.

- My life will improve when I stop waiting for a rescuer, and begin to rescue myself.

- I can learn to act in the best interests of a relationship without neglecting my own best interests.

- I can own my own power wherever I am, wherever I go, whomever I'm with.

- I will surround myself with people who are learning to live and enjoy their own lives.

- I can take responsibility for myself. I don't have to take responsibility for other people.

- I need love, but I don't need destructive love.

- Controlling keeps me from enjoying other people, and it blocks their growth.

Self-Esteem

- Being a victim is the path of least resistance.

- I can trust myself. I am wiser than I think.

- I will strive to be all that I can be.

- I'm the most important person in my universe.

- I can learn something worthwhile every day of my life.

- Life is not over till it's over.

- A strong person is not always big, but a big person is always strong.

Peace

- Walking on eggshells makes an irritating sound. I don't have to do it.

- Denial is when I pretend my circumstances are something other than what they are.

- I can learn to recognize when I'm reacting, rather than responding.

- When I've done all I can do, it's time to let go.

- When I'm feeling in chaos, I need to say and do as little as possible so I can restore my peace.

- I can ask for what I want and need. If I don't get it, I can figure out what to do next.

- Let go and let God.

- One day at a time.

- During stressful times, I can rely more heavily on my support system.

- Just for today, I will be strong enough to accept anything that comes my way.

- Today is the first day of the rest of my life.

- I will learn to use my head before I use my words.

* * *

Cut these suggestions out or write each one on a piece of paper and tape them to your bathroom mirror. Hopefully, you have a mirror large enough to hold all the wonderful new messages you will be taping over the next few months. Look through magazines, newspaper articles, and one-day-at-a-time calendars. Listen to other people's wisdom and if something strikes you with a ring of healthy truth, write it down and put it on your mirror. Every morning read your messages as you face yourself in the mirror. Little by little, you will be reprogramming yourself. Something magical happens with mirrors. It is as if you are literally taking these words of truth and planting them deep inside you. Like the childhood fairy tale *Mirror, Mirror on the Wall, Who's the Fairest of Them all*, in time, you will discover, *you are*. Treat these messages as valuable jewels, for the change they will bring has the highest value of anything you will ever acquire.

In times of stress, search your mirror for that particular truth that reflects the situation you are troubled about. As time goes on, you'll find that sooner or later, everything you need to get well will show up on that mirror. Your unconscious mind will begin searching throughout your day for what you need. Eventually you'll listen to what people who have wisdom say, and there, too, you will acquire words for your mirror, especially as you move across that bridge and begin spending time with people who are healthy.

There is an old Chinese proverb: *If you provide fish for a man, he will have food for a day; if you teach a man to fish, he will have food for life*. In building your Magic Mirror, you are giving yourself food for life.

Journaling

Writing your most private thoughts on paper on a daily basis is an excellent way to stay in touch with your inner self as well as an opportunity to access places that will illuminate the truth. You will need a safe place to store it. Without a sense of safety and privacy, you may find yourself editing and deleting thoughts that will bring you the most help. If your family members are not to be trusted, leave your journals with someone who is, until you are ready to confront a decision about your partner. There should be nothing too sacred or too personal for you to write about. Writing enables you to see the truth more clearly. Keep remembering the screaming child inside of you that is waiting for you to reach her or him. Treat your journal as if it is your best friend, one that can not only keep a confidence, but knows how to maintain silence when you want to speak.

Draw Pictures with Your Left Hand

Find a quiet time and a safe place. Gather crayons and blank sheets of paper. Whether you have talent or not, begin drawing pictures of your life, starting at the age of two, with your left hand (if you are right-handed. If you are left-handed, draw the pictures with your right hand). Draw at one-year intervals pictures of the first thing that comes into your mind. Use crayons to depict emotions—blue for sad times, black for grief, red for fear and anger, yellow and green for happiness. Let your mind float through the memories you draw. If you don't remember anything at that age, use your imagination from family stories you have heard to recreate a possible scene. Search through family photos and speak with relatives about events that happened when you were a child. Leave no stone unturned.

The unconscious mind stores an incredible amount of information, and what you draw based on other people's information may not be that far off. If you are utilizing the services of a competent therapist, take your pictures to your next session. The two of you can discuss their significance. If you are working without a therapist, choose a time when you are well-rested, have a full stomach, and are not in the middle of a stressful problem. Sit in a quiet place where you can examine each one. Write below the picture what you think it means, and how that particular scene has impacted your life now. If you have a safe family member who was a part of that scene, show the picture to them and get their input. It may prove invaluable.

Talk into a Recorder

You are now ready to travel through time in an even more revealing manner. Your smartphone may have a built-in voice-recording app or you can buy an Olympus voice recorder for under $20. Talk into the recorder about your life, your childhood, your feelings, your problems, and possible solutions. Talk about your hopes and wishes now, and what they were when you were little. Search through your life as if you were looking for missing pieces, for in truth, you are. Nothing is too unimportant to talk about.

Play the recording back and listen to everything you've said. Try to be fair-minded and realistic about what was abuse and what was not. If you can remember a time before your abuse happened, talk about that. Remember the good, the healthy parts to your childhood. Did you have an uncle who treated you with love and consideration? Talk about him. Was your grandmother nurturing and supportive? Remember her. Talk about the pain of all that happened whether it was related to your abuse or not. It will prove not only cathartic but you may find explanations for how you were set up to be molested. Drag all the ghosts into the light and look at them.

If it helps, label the PM (Pre Molestation) time and the AM (After Molestation) time. What you are trying to do is reach across the trauma to the time before it happened. That is where your inner child lives, waiting for you to get healthy. Eventually, you will need to connect the two of you. Talking to yourself and listening back to all that your life was will build a picture. There you will locate all the missing parts. Your life will then be complete. The use of your hand-held recorder will begin the healing process, exposing all the demons. Listening back is the key.

Hypnosis

Your parents may or may not have insurance that covers hypnotherapy. If somehow you can afford it, some of you may find it helpful, others not. For some victims, who have either no memory or only shadowy ones, hypnotherapy, coordinated with the efforts of your primary therapist, can be a great help. Hypnosis taps into the unconscious mind, the receptacle of all that has happened in your life. Not everyone is a candidate for this sort of therapy for a variety of reasons, and for those who aren't, it would aid them little. This is not usually discovered until you begin to undergo the actual hypnosis. But if you are receptive, it can be a tremendous aid in recapturing memories needed to see the complete picture.

The memories can be searing, so prepare to enter territory that will not be pleasant. It may not even be cleansing, but it will be revealing. Give thought as well as much discussion with your primary therapist before entering this realm. Weigh and balance the need for it. For some, it becomes the final argument that the abuse really happened and the one thing needed to surge ahead with the truth. For others, it brings to the fore realities they'd prefer not to have in their head. The choice is yours. Take into account the wisdom of your therapist before making that decision. When I mention "your therapist", I understand that as a teen ager who may not be confiding in anyone from their nuclear family regarding their recovery process, you may not have access to a therapist. Almost all schools have a school counselor; you might look into scheduling an appointment and include them in your REPAIR program. This is your call and is not vital, especially as all therapists are not created equal.

Making a List of Your Shame—Defining Healthy and Unhealthy

While you are in recovery, you will hear a lot about shame, that feeling of humiliation that stems from guilt. There are two different kinds of shame: healthy and unhealthy. Healthy shame, a result of your own actions, is a positive motivator. If you badmouth a friend in a moment of anger, the guilt prompts shame, which brings about a need for restitution and a restructuring of what you discuss. When you work your way through the Twelve-Steps, you will learn how to deal with healthy shame without feeling less of a person. As time goes on, you will see healthy shame as a valuable tool for removing negativity. In addition, it will give you the courage to face many day-to-day situations that used to cause you embarrassment. When combined with courage and assertiveness, it brings great strides in your confidence as well as the growth of your soul.

Unhealthy shame, on the other hand, is that secret part of you that feels such low self-worth that you become immobilized. No other word so aptly describes the one attribute that keeps child sexual abuse secret. This kind of shame is the direct result of other people's actions. As is usually the case, when dealing with the action of another, this one is more difficult to overcome and more painful. Instead of adjusting your behavior patterns to keep an uncomfortable event from repeating, you have to depend on an adjustment in others. Sometimes modifying your behavior will generate that adjustment, causing the shame to pass.

Shame caused by sexual abuse does not pass that easily. Upon that original shame, you build years of additional shame, locking it into that closet in your mind, until the burden becomes unbearable. Trying to live a healthy life while you are buried in shame is impossible. That shame is the infection that needs to be lanced. When someone belittles you in public or rebuffs a kindness in front of other students, shame crawls like a physical discomfort over your body. It tells something about them, not about you. However, untreated sexual abuse victims have such low self-worth that they are unable to see this. Once recovery is completed, your response to such actions comes from a place of strong self-esteem. You will be able to foil such opponents with "I" statements, such as "I'm sorry you feel that way. Perhaps we can talk privately once you are feeling better." The more you practice this, the easier it becomes. Eventually, you will almost welcome any challenge to your ability to turn a negative comment or action into a positive response. The resultant feeling of confidence empowers you. Personal power is one of the primary purposes of recovery. With that one quality, you can be and do anything you want.

Make a list of your shame, all those things you've done over the years that weigh heavily on your shoulders. Once you enter a Twelve-Step Program, you will be doing this in more detail. Some Twelve-Step programs have groups for teens only. Check with whichever Twelve-Step Program you may be interested in to see if they have any.

Don't just list the things you did; list what others have done to you. This exercise is to get your feet wet and begin seeing the results of what happened to you when you were younger. Mostly, it is an attempt to see the truth. Armed with this, you can begin making quantum leaps in self-confidence.

Things I've done that caused shame.

_____

_____

_____

_____

_____

Things others have done to me that caused me shame.

_____

_____

_____

_____

Things Others Have Done to Me that Caused Shame

The things you've done over the years that brought guilt are probably a direct result of being molested. Let this be your own examination of conscience. Don't be afraid. Confession really is good for the soul. An amazing thing happens once you face those demons. You live through it, and become stronger as a result. The more you write about your shame, the more it will diminish. Your esteem will grow in direct proportion to the release of your shame.

You need do nothing further than write it down. This is a cleansing process, and later on, if you go through a Twelve-Step program, you'll rid yourself of all of that shame. It was never yours to begin with and you will learn to place it squarely in the lap where it belongs—your perpetrator.

Attend Seminars

Many groups in your area provide help for childhood traumas. Check newspapers, college bulletin boards and check with your school counselor. Look for flyers at your Twelve-Step meetings that advertise seminars and groups. Check hospitals, churches, and doctor and therapist offices for other flyers. Recovery is everywhere.

You are fortunate, for never before at any time in the history of man, have so many options been available for mental and emotional health. A hundred years ago, there were no Twelve-Step programs, no therapists, no books available for recovery, and no John Bradshaw. Even fifty years ago, there were almost no tools to help with sexual abuse recovery, and post recovery was a term unheard of. As short a time as thirty years ago, there was still little help available for recovery. Therapists poked around in your brain with almost no answers and no desire to look at the hard subjects. A topic seldom discussed openly finds few opportunities to improve. Even today, one can find motion pictures filled with sex and violence that draw the public in droves, while movies with incest or other child sexual abuse as its central theme die a rapid death. The subject is too difficult and too shameful for most people to deal with. Our program, REPAIR, is a soft focus on that hard subject.

Remember, as we said earlier, that if you find yourself in a group or at a seminar that is beginning to feel uncomfortable, do not be afraid to walk away. Trust your inner voices; they do not lie. Not all recovery groups are healthy. They mean to, but are often misguided. Speak out when you are uncomfortable. If your questions are not answered to your satisfaction and you are still leery, leave and discuss your feelings and thoughts with your therapist or your Twelve-Step group where you'll feel safe.

If you feel you would like to start a Lamplighter chapter, check their website at **www.thelamplighters.org** and under the *Start a Group In Your Area*, you'll find a link to the Lamplighter Facilitator Guide, which explains how incredibly easy it is to start a chapter. Check first to see if there is already a Lamplighter Chapter in your area. The website has a list of the location of chapters.

Work a Rigorous Twelve-Step program

Working the Twelve Steps, while not vital to making your way across the bridge, is a tremendous help. For almost seventy years, they have a proven track record to be almost miraculous in their recovery rate. But it is not sufficient to just attend meetings. Only in working the steps, one after another in the order in which they were designed will you receive their full benefit.

Take your time. It may be as much as a year or longer before you work your way through the first. But you will find as you proceed, that they get easier, not harder. Each one is designed to build strength and prepare you for the next. If you have ever heard anyone describe the "spiritual awakening" you receive at Step Twelve, you too will want to make your way to that step. It is an incredible experience that can only be felt after completing the other eleven steps.

Another way of accessing help is in finding a sponsor. This is a fellow Twelve-Stepper who has already been through the program and is willing to guide you as you do your own Twelve-Step work. Utilizing the services of a sponsor is a personal choice. Some function fine with only a therapist as a guide, and others will need a sponsor. If you don't have a therapist, you will probably need a sponsor. Part of the tradition in Twelve-Steps is to reach out to others with help as needed as well. If you feel comfortable about it, write down phone numbers from the other members and utilize the network you create for a support group that can clearly identify with what you are going through. Others, uncomfortable with this, are more loners. There again, it is a personal choice. Each of you is different and this may be another part of your own rhythm, a topic we will discuss later. Check your library and/or bookstores. You will find a wealth of media and books that prove excellent guides in working your way through the steps. You are never alone in any part of this program. In addition, many Twelve-Step meetings provide literature free of charge, or at a minimal cost.

Create a Family History

Creating a family history is an important part of your recovery. Through it, you will see a pattern that helps to access the truth. Once you discover the dysfunctional family members that are a part of your history, you'll understand that raising a healthy child with those tools was an impossible task. A grandfather who was a womanizer would definitely have sent wrong messages to his children. A grandmother who was an adult-child (an adult who never went through all the developmental stages while growing up that are necessary to be a fully functioning adult) paired with a patriarchal husband would have developed codependent ways. If she had alcoholic brothers that she coddled and made excuses for, the lineage who witnessed this would have an incorrect concept of how healthy being an alcoholic really is. The list goes on and on. Once you follow your generations back through time, you'll discover that you were an accident waiting to happen. The power of this knowledge is in the realization that it wasn't your fault. You were set up.

Fig. 5-2: Understand Your Family Tree

1. List all members of your nuclear (birth) family, starting with the oldest (parents) down to the youngest. Include yourself.

_____

_____

_____

2. List mother's parents. _____

                          _____

3. List father's parents. _____

                          _____

4. List any aunts or uncles, grandfathers or grandmothers who lived with your birth family during your growing-up years.

_____

_____

_____

5. List any known boundary violation behavior patterns that any family members may have exhibited, i.e., fondling inappropriate parts of your body, lewd suggestions and/or inappropriate remarks, etc. (no matter how minor) and who it was.

_____

_____

_____

6. List any comments you may have heard over the years regarding any of the above family members that would indicate they had boundary violation behavior patterns. Example: in my case, the well-known comment about my paternal grandfather was, "No woman is safe with him."

_____

_____

_____

7. List any known sex offenders in the family, whether criminally prosecuted or not. If none, write "not applicable."

_____

_____

_____

8. Draw (using stick figures if necessary) the history of your family. Mark the members with inappropriate boundary violations with a red color. Mark yourself with a blue one. Draw a circle around the ones that could have protected you but didn't for whatever reason. Draw yourself in the middle and the others in varying degrees of closeness to you.

* * *

Creating a family history may entail calling relatives to ask questions. Some will be cooperative, others not. Explain honestly what you are going through and the help you need. Pay close attention to any revelations concerning unhealthy behavior of your parents, grandparents, and great-grandparents. Go as far back as you need. If letters are available, study them. You'd be surprised what the written words of others reveal about their inner selves. Often people will put on paper what they don't have the courage to speak out loud. Act as if you were a reporter gathering information for a story. In a way you are—yours.

Write a letter (to your perpetrator and your parents—if you feel they betrayed you by not protecting you.)

Don't be afraid to write down everything that is inside of you. By now, from reading books, journaling, listening to MP3s or CDs, doing some of the exercises, and talking into your voice recorder, a picture is emerging. You will have a lot to share. In doing this, you will be taking the shame off your shoulders and laying it squarely where it belongs. This exercise will cause a lightening of the heart. Once you give something away, it is no longer yours.

If parents/perpetrators are deceased, travel to their graves. Sit on the earth and have a heart-to-heart talk about the pain and the shame which was handed to you so many years ago. Get angry. Speak out loud about what their actions cost you. Leave nothing untouched. This will prove to be the catharsis that allows you to forgive and let go of the past.

By now you've taken on a lot of work for yourself. It may or may not be weighing heavily on you. We hope it is beginning to help you feel a lightening of the heart. On the next page are some tips to help you as you go through this period.

Tips To Help You in the Midst of Your Journey

Remember HALT: Hungry Angry Lonely Tired. Whenever you are having difficulty coping, remember to check this list. If any one of these is present, taking care of those needs will bring immediate emotional relief.

The Attitude of Gratitude—Daily list all your blessings in your mind. Everyone has some even though they may seem unimportant. Do you like to read? How about the movies? How about a special friend? Do you have lovely hands? A high energy level? Are you warm and affectionate? Do you like your job? If not, do you like your co-workers? Dig, dig, dig. You will find many more than you realized. Write them down. Something magical happens. Your blessings will begin to increase. And as they increase, so will your optimism about life and all its promises. These blessings will be an oasis in the midst of your journey across that bridge.

Create your own repertoire of "courage songs." Throughout the ages, people have adopted songs that gave them courage to keep living no matter how dark the times looked. Songs like *From A Distance* (Bette Midler), *Keep Your Head Up* (Andy Grammer), *Bigger Than My Body* (John Mayer), *Uncertainty* (Natasha Beddingfield), *Are You Who You Want To Be?* (Switchfoot), *Fly* (Hilary Duff), and *Born This Way* (Lady Gaga) are courage songs. The songs are stirring, give us hope, and bind us to a promise. Find some of your own and whether you sing or not, use the words to give you courage. You will be surprised how much stronger you'll feel.

Listen to John Bradshaw's recordings—over and over.

Pamper yourself—by indulging in something that makes you feel good: an evening walk, lunch with a friend, buy flowers for no reason, schedule a massage therapy or spa visit, curl up with a good book, write a letter to someone you love telling them how well you are doing and all the new things you're learning.

Write a letter to your inner child—that "small you" who is waiting for the two of you to meet.

Take your life one day at a time, one hour at a time, and, if necessary, one minute at a time.

Call a supportive friend and share everything you're feeling.

Make a "wish list" of all you want to do with the rest of your life. Don't worry about whether it's realistic or not, just write it down. When you begin asking the universe for your dreams, it starts paying attention, for the world loves persistence and rewards those who practice it.

Learning To Deal With the Trust Issue

One of the most anguishing results of being sexually violated at a young age is the betrayal of trust. An unspoken understanding in the universe is that when one gives birth to a child, one is responsible for their wellbeing and must take that challenge seriously. Unfortunately, not everyone does. When a child is born, they look to their parents for protection against any unpleasantness. When the parent is either the perpetrator of unpleasantness or the unwilling partner to its happening by virtue of doing nothing, it is a betrayal. One of the by-products is a child who grows up unable to trust those around them. Why should they? The world has become a scary place where they wish everyone wore a black or white hat, depending on what role they are playing. Unfortunately they don't.

How does one cope with the inability to trust? Learning to differentiate between the bad guys and the good guys is a step in this direction. Setting boundaries buys you time to gain more information, enabling you to do this. Relying on your own inner voices is another. Learning to place the blame for that mistrust where it belongs is a third. As you move through this program, these things will happen. As your own emotional and mental maturity develops, you will gain the confidence needed to make choices that impact whether or not you are in a safe place. Practice will eventually enable you to remove yourself from any situation that reeks of potential harm. Taking your time in getting to know others will add to your feeling of safety. Much of this will come together when we arrive at the AWARENESS part of our program.

Boundary Setting

Once you cross that bridge you will be ready to empower yourself. You are going to learn a sense of restraint. It will not be easy in the beginning. Like any new behavior, practice makes perfect. As you grow in confidence and your self-esteem increases, having a sense of restraint will in time become second nature. The immediate gratification that so many wounded children go through will begin to feel like downright foolishness, especially when you count up the many times it got you in trouble. Being a victim is about giving your power and control to another. Curbing your impulses (restraint) is about giving yourself that power.

Think about ways to empower yourself with boundaries. Examples: Buy a shirt that says *What part of NO don't you understand?* Wear it often, especially around those who try to control you. If you can't find one, put the words on your Magic Mirror so you will be reminded to use them when others try to wear you down with their own persistence. Practice saying "no". Simple statements such as, "Why do you ask?" or "That's kind of a personal question," are great for setting boundaries. "I'll get back to you," or "Let me think about it," are ways to stall people who demand instant answers and ask questions that are too

Fig. 5-4: Healthy Boundaries are Good for Everyone

personal. Give yourself time before making decisions. You have the right to take as much time as you want. No one has the right to bully or manipulate you into responding to their needs. Learn to recognize the signs of manipulative and controlling people: passive/aggressive behavior, game playing, whining, laying guilt trips, and dragging out "old stuff" that have already been resolved, are only a few of their tactics. If you do not respond, they will soon give up. Unhealthy behaviors like these require more than one person to play.

Do not give away your power. You have earned it. *Get stubborn* about your own rights. No one else's demands are anywhere near as important as your own. We're not talking about selfishness; we're talking about survival.

Boundary setting will encourage a child sexual abuse person to deal in a healthy manner with one of the most prominent emotional difficulties they have—anger. Being angry at your perpetrator is not only normal, but healthy. At the time of your original trauma, you weren't able to feel the anger, much less deal with it. As years go by, the anger has accelerated until nothing short of murder feels comfortable. It's time to deal with the anger. If for no other reason, holding onto anger can cause serious physical ailments. Unresolved conflicts—anger is one—turn inward. Once they turn inward, you are forcing your body to deal with the emotional pain and it will not have enough energy to deal with your physical health. Your immune system will weaken. Are you willing to give your perpetrator (and the anger you feel) the power to damage—perhaps permanently—your body? Who would win in the end? Certainly not you.

Letting go of your anger is vital to the healing process. As you learn boundary setting, you will feel stronger. Feeling stronger alleviates some of the anger. Knowing that you cannot go back and change what happened but that you can go forward into a healing mode helps. Once you see the overall picture, especially the family history, it will be easier to approach this step.

Make a list of ways to create boundaries.

I will empower myself by:

_____

_____

_____

_____

_____

Turning to your minister/priest

If you belong to a church and feel comfortable about it, schedule a talk with your minister/priest. Not all clergy will be supportive or may not be supportive in the way you hoped for. It's amazing how many people (and you may or may not have already experienced this with your nuclear family, if you have confided in them) will tell you to just forget it, to not bring it up again, or will respond with rage that you would even be doing this. If your perpetrator is your father, your brother may not believe your father is capable of such a deed. It's amazing how many people will respond with shame for you, anger at you, extreme discomfort that you would even bring the subject up, and so on. That is sad. That is also one of the reasons that child sexual abuse is so prevalent and is difficult to eradicate.

"To Feel is to Heal"

Some of you feel you have cried enough tears to drown the world. You may have. Others have been living in a shell of stony emotions all their lives, unable to feel even the good. If you never cried before, you will learn to do so now. Whether you cried before or not, the tears you have now will not be of anger, fear, and frustration, but tears of genuine sorrow—a healing kind of sorrow. As you move through the pain, as you see the complete picture, and especially, as you meet your inner child, all the feelings will contribute to bringing together that fragmented part of yourself that exploded at the moment of trauma.

Learn to identify feelings you're having. Periodically, throughout your day, ask yourself *what am I feeling right now?* In time, this will arm you with reality on what is the appropriate response for each situation that occurs. Anger requires setting boundaries; fear involves finding a supportive friend to share it with, or going with the saying: "Feel the fear and do it anyway". Other responses may be: wise insights on why you're afraid and what you can do to offset it; joy promotes wellbeing and illustrates more clearly that life is good; and so on. Identifying feelings and their appropriate responses not only empowers and strengthens you, it has the added reward of making you feel centered and stable. The more you do this, the more it will become second nature.

Meeting Your Inner Child

What lies behind us and what lies before us
Are tiny matters compared to what lies within us.

When Oliver Wendell Holmes wrote those words, the concept of the inner child was still part of the future. The power of that which lies within us, which includes your inner child, is an awesome one. You are now ready to meet that lost child who has been waiting all these years for you to realize she exists. Start by collecting family photos of yourself at a young age, in particular of the time before you were violated. Study them. Put them next to your bed where you can see them upon awakening. Look at them frequently and as you do, try to remember what you were doing and what took place at the time the photo was taken. If you can't remember, create a memory; it may not be that far off. Sometimes talking to supportive family members about photos from the past will jog their memory and give you more information.

Choose a place where you may have spent happy time as a child: a park, a playground, a beach, an empty field, etc. If you had none, create one in your mind. Being near things of God (Mother Nature) will help you in this. Close your eyes and sit quietly. Travel back in your mind through the years until you arrive at that place where your inner child dwells. Think about what it must be like to once be happy and carefree and then be locked in a prison. Picture being frightened and alone as a child inside the mind and body of a grown up. Picture that child wanting desperately for the grown-up part of her to acknowledge her existence.

Slowly, your child will step out of the shadows. This will not happen overnight. You may spend weeks at that park, waiting for your inner child to come forth. He or she has spent years in hiding and needs to learn to trust that you are serious about bringing her into a safe place. Why should they come out to meet you only to find more pain waiting?

Once your inner child sees that you are doing everything in your power to turn your life around, they'll be ready. Reach out and embrace them. Tell them you love them and you are sorry to have turned your back on them all these years. Weep with them for all the sad times. Then let them know that you are working on getting well and that one day, they will stop crying; they will be free and happy.

For the next few weeks, spend time with that inner child in your place of happy childhood memories. Talk with them about all that happened—all the despairing times, no matter how small. As they tread painfully through each, give them a hug and tell them that while you weren't there for them then, you are now. Bond with that inner child in your mind as much as you can. You are taking missing pieces of your life and connecting them as you would create the picture from pieces to a puzzle. As you do this exercise, you will remember things you had long forgotten. Assembling these pictures will eventually make you a whole person, instead of fragmented. Eventually, as the months pass, you will one day realize that your inner child is now the same age as you. When this happens, it brings great inner strength and personal power.

You are now ready to enter the next step, Awareness.

Fig. 5-5: Meet Your Inner Child!

Awareness

Understanding is the key,

Acceptance is the door.

Socrates, one of the world's greatest philosophers, once said, "An unexamined life is not worth living." Much truth lies in those words as well as much power. In this chapter, you will need to draw on this to understand the importance of *Awareness*.

The quality of becoming aware includes many components. Sensibility, prudence, knowledge, visualization, feeling, and foresight are a few. They are siblings in the same family, gifts given to humans at birth. With these gifts, a human can be and do all to which they aspire. Let's take a closer look at these qualities before we proceed to see what part they played in your childhood sexual abuse issue.

Properties of Awareness

Sensibility	Visualization
Prudence	Feeling
Knowledge	Foresight

Sensibility

One of the marks of sensibility is the capacity to reason, to use your head and think things through. It is an invaluable tool to have by your side as you journey through life. A sensible person makes wiser decisions. He doesn't react; he responds. He knows he can take all the time in the world to make a choice, and because he can, he makes the best choice possible.

Prudence

Without reason or sensibility, one cannot have prudence. Prudence is cautious, not headstrong and impulsive. Prudence doesn't get one in situations that leave scars, because it's skilled in good judgment and knows all the resources available. Prudence uses that reason to discipline itself, and once disciplined, life falls into order rather than chaos. One finds peace and tranquility in that order.

Knowledge

Knowledge gathers experiences and sorts through them for the right answers. Knowledge is cognizant of the full range of truths available in one's life. Knowledge investigates, observes, and studies not only human nature, but the nature of things and the nature of the universe. In gathering knowledge, one gains power, especially personal power.

Visualization

The ability to see all that you know, bringing it to life so that you can choose your next step, is a rare but not impossible quality. Vision, throughout the ages, has progressed men from the humblest backgrounds to some of the greatest positions on earth. On a smaller scale, visualization forms mental images that propel you into your dreams. Without visualization, you have no dreams. Create a vision; then step into it.

Feeling

The capacity to respond emotionally to everything that happens in your life is a strength, not a weakness. People who are aware of what is happening in their universe can feel. Feelings bond you to others, give you drive, protect you against wrongs, and offer the gifts of humor, pathos, joy, and sorrow. Even sorrow has a healing property necessary to becoming a whole person. It is not feelings that get people in trouble; it is the actions they take based on those feelings.

Foresight

This simple act of looking forward takes you from the past to the present and into the future. You can do nothing about what has gone before; but the present, although elusive and shifting, is the arena of change. Healthy choices made in the now will open a future that promises the fulfillment of your God-given potential.

* * *

Now let's take a look at these Awareness gifts inherent to man and see where they fit into the life of a person who was sexually abused as a child. They don't. When you're living in a world filled with chaos and trauma, moving from one crisis to another, the sibling qualities of Awareness can do little good.

Sensibility—How can a person filled with despair begin to put pieces together to find answers that make sense?

Prudence—Once sexually molested, reacting, rather than responding to the daily events in your life is the only tool you know to use, thereby eliminating prudence. Good judgment is a luxury you cannot afford.

Knowledge—One who is sexually abused as a child may instinctively know the answers but is unable to follow through with the right choices. Knowledge only becomes a powerful tool when utilized in conjunction with the other properties of Awareness.

Visualization—Who can see anything but hopelessness when all you hear is a child screaming inside of you—when all you know is that nothing ever works out for you?

Feeling—The wounded child has plenty of feelings, all of them either out of control or locked into that closet in their mind for fear that, once unleashed, would be uncontrollable.

Foresight—The emotional growth of a child who has been sexually abused is locked in time at the moment of their trauma. There is no foresight for them, for they see no future, only a despairing past and a chaotic present.

This is what child sexual abuse has done—robbed you of these six God-given rights. It is our hope that by the time you arrive at this part of REPAIR, you will begin to experience the joy that the components of Awareness brings. They come little by little. One day you realize that you just set a boundary to give yourself time to make a decision. Knowledge combined with prudence and accompanied by foresight gave you a useful tool. What a great step! It's time for another.

Your decisions seem wiser, partially a result of sensibility. Your old friends (those whose own lives are consumed with the same chaos and despair you used to have), annoyed at you for not being "yourself", begin to fall away. As they do so, an amazing thing happens. You don't miss them. You'll begin to realize that you're on a different road now and you have nothing in common. You'll also begin making friends that are on the same road, thereby enhancing your ability to complete REPAIR.

As you move through the program and assemble the pieces to your life, a picture emerges—the pieces to the puzzle that your life has become.

Now it's time to take a look at the other common denominators of a child who has been sexually abused, the family systems factors. This is the forest that your trees (the individual common denominators) grew under. In order to assemble the puzzle, check which of the following family systems' common denominators fit into your picture.

Family System Checklist	
Patriarchal (or matriarchal) family system	
Obedient/co-dependent mother (father)	
Religiously regimented household	
Eldest daughter	
Alcoholic (or other addicted) parent: Mother [ ] Father [ ]	
Family history of sexual boundary violators	

Write a few words about how you think any checked item impacted your life while you were growing up. Was it positive or negative? In which way?

_____

_____

_____

_____

_____

_____

Write about how you think it changed your behavior as an adult.

_____

_____

_____

_____

_____

_____

Now, let's take a look at each one.

Patriarchal (or Matriarchal) Family

Most dysfunctional families have both a strong link and a weak one. In a home where sexual abuse occurs, the strong link is usually the father, if the home is patriarchal by nature; the mother, if it's matriarchal. The supremacy of the father or mother goes a long way toward promoting obedience, the primary quality needed to be a victim of child sexual abuse. The common denominator here is someone in a position of power who has the character defect of abusing that power.

The weak link is the victim, the child who has been trained almost from birth to do what she is told without question. An obedient child is a sitting duck for a perpetrator.

In a healthy environment, a child learns discipline, not obedience. She is encouraged to be able to say "no"—to speak her mind, to have her own ideas, concepts, goals, and personality. Thereby she is able to grow, not only physically, mentally, spiritually, and emotionally, but in maturity as well. Even in a patriarchal family, the head of the household has responsibilities, not power. In a healthy environment, he (or she) provides guidance, knowledge, wisdom, caring, and discipline.

In an unhealthy environment, that weak link is exposed to situations where anything other than total obedience is punishable. The child is no match for the power of the patriarch. As the patriarch continues to be obeyed, his power grows; for that which we feed becomes a monster. Fed by this enormous ego, the perpetrator pushes through any boundaries a child/victim could even begin to set as well as any accepted rules of the society in which he lives. Keep in mind that even if your perpetrator was a sibling, an uncle, a grandfather, or some other family member, these patterns still apply. Only your perpetrator is different.

Are you the child of a patriarchal (or matriarchal) home? Does your patriarch abuse his responsibilities? List situations other than your sexual abuse where you were powerless as a child.

_____

_____

_____

_____

_____

Obedient/Co-Dependent Mother (Father) with Weak Boundaries

[This parent may or may not have been sexually violated themselves.] All positives have a negative, each yin has a yang; and so the patriarchal father (or mother) usually has an obedient partner. Frequently in the life of a child who has been sexually abused, that partner was also an untreated sexual abuse victim, who has weak boundaries and is so wounded that they are unable to protect their child or fight back against the patriarch.

Every family has unspoken rules. Prior to the 1960s, most families had an unspoken value system that proclaimed, "The father makes the decisions; is the ruler of all that happens in this house; the mother carries out his orders and sees to it that the value system is perpetuated." In the 1940s, one of the unspoken rules regarding the patriarch was, "Even when he's wrong, he's right." They lived and died by this rule. So deeply ingrained were these rules that even seeing the reality of their own child being used for sexual purposes by their husband was not strong enough for most women to break through that obedient state and protect their child. Sometimes, turning against the child was safer.

The following is a checklist of codependent behavior.

Co-dependency Symptoms Checklist	
They place other people's needs above their own.	
They are afraid to set and keep boundaries.	
They allow their mate to control them.	
They are afraid to ask for what they need.	
They are afraid to say what they're feeling.	
They are the giver in the relationship. This makes them angry.	
They are unhappy in the relationship and feel trapped.	
They hate the idea of solitude.	
They feel rejected if their mate spends time away from them.	
Unable to control their own pain, they try to control everyone around them.	

Did your mother or father have any traits from this list?

Write about how it felt to have a parent like this. Do *you* have any of the above traits?

Religiously Regimented Household

One of the most frequent common denominators of child sexual abuse victims (especially in the case of incest) is that of growing up in a religiously regimented household. We are not speaking of a spiritual environment. We are talking about one that contains a strong element of hypocrisy. This false appearance creates incredible confusion in a child. A confused child is a weakened child. A weakened child is easy prey. Regimentation requires rigidity as its primary element, and when you grow up in an environment that lacks flexibility, you have no opportunity for growth. The child who cannot grow because of the unyielding and inflexible core contained in his family loses not only his freedom but becomes locked in a world where he has no knowledge of the truth. Without the truth, you have no life of your own; you literally become a puppet or a pawn on a chessboard.

Religious training that requires rigidity also fosters control. Armed with control and a lack of flexibility, the perpetrator sets up total obedience as the only choice with which the child can respond. When you add the reality that that same child places their perpetrator on a pedestal, you now have an almost hopeless situation.

Idolizing a perpetrator at an early age is a mental attitude that follows into adulthood, especially if its origin lies in a religiously regimented household. That perpetrator represents God. We don't know how not to idolize them. And so we speak of them in larger-than-life terms. "He was so handsome that women swooned; his talent as a pianist exceeded all else; we thought he was God;" etc. etc. are common statements made by victims about their perpetrators once they reach adulthood. Often, they have a lifelong need to find another they can place on a pedestal. Seeing people as they really are is difficult. If they could realistically see their partners, they would not make such unhealthy choices in that area. In order to change this behavior, it is important to first see your perpetrator clearly. This is difficult, but not impossible.

As unbelievable as it may seem, if his sexual needs were not being met, the potential perpetrator in a religiously regimented household would not commit adultery. That is a sin against the sixth commandment. But sleeping with your daughter is not. The old joke about incest being all right as long as you keep it in the family, despite being said in jest, is another of the unspoken rules.

What is saddest of all is the loss of that spirituality you might have obtained had you been raised in a family that valued the golden rule and not the hell-and-damnation code they lived by. What chance does a child in this family have to fight back or to develop their own innate sense of goodness?

Were you raised in such a household? Was God a fearful God? Did he wear a face similar to your perpetrator? How did your perpetrator use religion as a whip to crack you into obedience? What would your life have been like in a spiritual nest rather than a controlled religious environment? Write about these things.

Read your own answers back. If it helps, use your voice recorder rather than your pen. The important thing is the words—these words will tap into the truth and the truth will set you free.

Oldest Daughter

At a young age, the oldest daughter often becomes a mother figure. Being in charge of younger siblings encourages caretaking, and caretaking is one of the qualities of a codependent. In a healthy environment, this ability to care for others is a virtue that is tempered with maturity and strong boundaries. In a family with incest, the oldest daughter loses herself in her struggle to assume adult responsibilities she is not prepared for. All growth comes in stages. An oldest daughter who is not allowed her childhood becomes a mother symbol in the perpetrator's mind. She is now ripe for his sexual desires.

If you add to this picture the same daughter as a housekeeper, you have a person with the blueprint of an adult. As she becomes an adolescent, her budding sexuality tantalizes and tempts the perpetrator. He no longer sees her as his little girl.

Alcoholic/Addicted Father or Mother

While medical science is proving that genetics plays a large part in alcoholism, other factors come into play as well. The alcoholic is hiding a tremendous amount of pain, most of which no doubt stemmed from his or her own childhood trauma. More than likely, your alcoholic parent was not the first one in your family history. Statistics prove that the number of alcoholics as you go back generation after generation is enormous; in some families, almost epidemic. Heredity is a tendency, not a doom. Studies show that over 80% of substance abusers get intoxicated as a form of self-medication. The very nature of alcoholism prohibits healthy behavior. In addition, the boundaries of an alcoholic are non-existent. They too may have been molested as a child, compounding their problem, and the debris that followed in its wake. If you came from an alcoholic family, the flip side was the codependent other half. You now have two common denominators in the profile of a molested person.

A Family History that Includes Boundary Violators

All families have skeletons in their closets. If you traveled back in time far enough, you would no doubt see at least one in every generation. This is the flawed side to human nature. No incest perpetrator arrived at his place without help. When you have children who raise children, you have an adult child. When you have a womanizer that raises a child, you create the potential for another womanizer, and so on. You are that which you have been trained to become not only with the blatant, spoken messages, but with subliminal ones as well. The subliminal ones are often more insidious. One person with unhealthy behavior can be responsible for decades of unhealthy descendants.

It only takes one person to break that cycle. Man has an enormous potential for goodness. But like a tree that is not pruned, watered, and fertilized, and does not face the sun, a child without the right guidance will become wounded and pass the results of their wounds to their children, their grandchildren, and their children.

The chance of a boundary violator lurking in your history is great. Seek them out. Write about them. Drag them out of the holes in which they hide and expose them. Label them for what they are. If your grandfather, so idolized by his children, was a womanizer, call him so. If your father, placed on a pedestal by those who knew him, sexually violated you, he needs to be toppled. Only in the seeking and finding of the truth will you be able to make an honest appraisal of your total picture.

* * *

Now you are ready to begin assembling the pieces. This brings you to the stage we are currently working on—Awareness. Find a safe place and some quiet time to meditate on all you have learned. Take a hard look, especially at the family history you have discovered. Think about the unhealthy messages and all the times in your life when you didn't have a choice. Would you have chosen differently if you could? Ask yourself searing questions and give yourself strong and sensible answers. How responsible are you for the actions of others? Tell yourself over and over: *This is a statement about them, not about me.*

Picture a chessboard with all its pieces. The pawn (you as a child) is moved and motivated strictly for the self-serving interests of the king and queen (your parents and/or your perpetrator). Significant aspects to the profile of an incest family may include many things. They are all red flags. How many red flags did you have on the *Profile Of A Child Sexual Abuse Victim* that you filled out earlier? How many did you want and would you have chosen at birth? How many showed up on your *Family Systems* profile?

Now, approach this puzzle from another perspective. What if no sexual abuse had happened as a child and your years had been all that you had wanted when you were younger? What would that picture have looked like? Would you now be confident and happy? Would you now have no dark shadows lingering in your head? Would you be getting good grades in school, have only healthy people as friends, and if you were dating, would your choice be supportive, kind, and loving? Would you be looking forward to college and have an idea where your place in the world would be? How much has the world lost in producing so many wounded children? That tiny child who was molested at the age of eight and lived a life of despair may have become a famous scientist who discovered a cure for cancer. That lovely daughter who was raped at the age of twelve may have been a renowned ballerina. Whether the molestation happened at the age of one or the age of seventeen, the trauma, unless interrupted by a strong recovery program, creates an indelible blueprint that follows their entire life.

Make a list of all that your life so far would have been if the trauma of sexual abuse had never impacted it. Where would you be today if this had turned out to be true? Probably not reading this book. It is not too late to have anything on your list. Remember that growing older can often be less a hindrance and more a help to your dreams. If you became wiser, more mature, more disciplined, and focused, couldn't you now go to college if that had been one of the things on your list? Once you complete this program, you'll become that person. If you now could tell the bad guys from the good ones, wouldn't you make a healthier choice in who you dated and who you have as friends? It's not too late. It's only too late when you say it is.

Richard Nixon once said, "A man is not finished when he's defeated; he's finished when he quits." Do you want to quit? Do you really want to be in the final years of your life and know that you had the opportunity to turn your life around and you failed to grasp it? Do you, especially, want to have children who will be raised by a stable, healthy, confident parent?

It's a proven fact that *Child molesters pick the most obedient child in the school yard.* As you progress further into recovery, you begin to understand this. You see yourself as that pawn in a game of chess, realizing you could not have changed your family history or the part you played in it.

List traits and behavior patterns you had prior to being molested; then list those you had as a result of being molested.

Traits before being molested	Traits after being molested

You are now ready for the next stage in REPAIR—the stage called Insight.

Insight

Freedom—A state man has struggled to attain throughout the centuries—

Is hindered only by the locks and prisons in our own mind.

At you move through the stages of REPAIR, what was lost in your life becomes clearer with every day that passes, as well as the desire to regain it. The Twelve Steps start to make sense; old messages are difficult to access; new ones spring out automatically. Your memory opens with things formerly hidden or lost. In the stage of Awareness, you assembled pieces to the puzzle that your life had become. It is time to put the pieces together so you can see the complete picture and comprehend what previously was obscure.

What you have been doing up to now, whether you realize it or not, is healing. Your fragile ego has not only been in a weakened condition, it has been battered. With little faith in yourself, you often do your own battering. As you proceed through the process of REPAIR, you slowly strengthen your self-esteem. Now you realize you are not to blame. Over the years, your perpetrator, like Pontius Pilate washing his hands, either directly or indirectly, placed the blame for **his** wrongdoing on you.

One of the ways in which he accomplished this purpose was through the use of subliminal messages. Subliminal messages have diabolical power and take root even more than blatant ones. If your perpetrator was your father, his subliminal message could have been, *It's okay to sleep with married men.* This may have be one of the directions you will take as an adult, thereby breeding self-loathing. It is difficult to have healthy self-esteem when you feel you are covered with garbage. Another one may have been, *It's not okay to set sexual boundaries.* What subliminal messages planted themselves in your unconscious, paving the way for unhealthy behavior?

Subliminal Messages Behaviors I Adopted As A Result

Subliminal Messages	Behaviors I Adopted As A Result

You were literally programmed to acquire a belief system at an early age that wasn't yours. The truth has a way of making sense, and as you moved through this program, truth became insightful.

Not all common denominators of sexual abuse were yours. You may even have others not previously mentioned in this book. The inability to appreciate physical contact, sometimes even to the point of aversion, can be another.

Don't worry if your traits were fewer in number than others. You have enough of them to be moving through this program for the right reasons. Not everyone is the same, nor is your reaction to things that happen in your life. One person can have suffered the most severe abuse imaginable and struggled through it to live a healthy life. Still others may have had what they consider minimal abuse and are crippled from it. The by-law here is the impact your particular trauma had on YOU.

A variety of reasons can contribute to the intensity that you felt in being abused. Human nature is a complex structure of many things. Some are more sensitive than others. Some are cursed (or blessed, as the case may be) with vivid recall. Still others have the ability to automatically detach from whatever is happening and skim over the top of the pain of their trauma. Analytical people are not as rooted in their pain as those with a creative and/or sensitive nature.

Are these people blessed? For some, it is a blessing. Others may have missed the intensity of the pain; but they have also missed the intensity of the joy of the good things that happened. And despite the pain of childhood sexual abuse, we all have had joyful moments. Each of us is unique; our differences are what makes the world such an exciting place in which to be. Work within your own parameters and don't attempt to walk another's path or judge another's journey.

The insight acquired by working this program will prompt you to establish a whole new belief system—your own. Along with that, you'll seek out mature behavior patterns. Test your own ability to recognize new-found maturity. Some examples are: *I will not judge until I have all the evidence; When I am wrong, I will apologize; My behavior will be gracious even towards those of whom I'm not fond; I will remember that life is too short to be little,* etc. List some of your own and those you would like to adopt.

Mature Behavior Patterns

The next time opportunity presents itself, practice by using one of your own mature behavior patterns. Then step back and see whether it improved the situation or not. In most cases, you will be pleasantly surprised. Find someone as a mentor whose maturity you admire. Watch their responses to life's problems and how they arrived at them. Explain that you would like their help in learning what they know. Perhaps they too once had a mentor and are happy to give their knowledge to others. This is one of the reasons why our world, especially in the area of mental health, is a better place to be in than it was a hundred years ago.

An important part of the essential nature of insight is your intuition—the part of us that knows and sees all truth. As you approach the end of your bridge, it will come to the foreground of your awareness level. This quality is called "listening to your inner voices". You all have them and the more you listen, the more they speak. They are all wise and all-knowing. There is no answer you need to know that is not contained in your inner voices. As you pass through life, everything that occurs feeds into your unconscious. It may lay in wait for many years before it is utilized, but when called upon to give a command performance, the truth presents itself. But how can you hear the truth when your life is consumed with distractions, especially unhealthy ones?

From birth, you are all trained to have distractions in your life. Some are necessary, but some are just ways to avoid tapping into one of your greatest resources: the inner voice—that intuition. How many people do you know that are obsessive talkers—talk, talk, talk? That way they don't have to connect with their inner child. How about obsessive television watchers—noise, noise, noise? It is an easy way to not only drown out the inner voices, but to distract yourself from that which you need to see to turn your life around. People who were molested have an even larger propensity for creating distractions in their lives. The greater the pain of your trauma, the greater your need for distractions to keep from feeling and seeing not only the intensity of the pain, but the consequences it brings.

You all need those occasional distractions that put balance in your life. A continual diet of examining your own behavior would become burdensome after a while. You need social interactions, fun activities, and goal-oriented projects in all areas to give you a balanced life. Growth in the area of the six dimensions—mental, emotional, physical, spiritual, social, and financial—is necessary for a stable and fulfilling life.

Little by little, as you work through REPAIR, you begin automatically to move away from the distractions and face the pain. As you do so, you also find healthy ways to combat the discomfort. Going to a therapy session that was particularly searing is followed by a movie you'd been looking forward to. It placed balance in the midst of an emotionally fragile time. Previously, you had no tools to apply ointment to the opening of these wounds. As you adopt these new and healthier behavior patterns, a surprising thing happens: you start feeling good about yourself. You begin feeling stronger. How did it happen? You have been moving not only across that bridge, but out of the dark and into the light. The ugly things waiting behind you seem further and further away. Dragons and demons lying in wait in the swirling waters under the bridge no longer frighten you. Of course, they don't, for you have become stronger. You did so by recognizing that the sexual abuse was not about you. It was about your perpetrator.

Somewhere during this realization of the truth, you hit a wall. Mom and Dad were not perfect. What a ghastly shock. You placed your life in their hands and trusted that they would guide you appropriately. Not only did they not, but sometimes you have to face the reality that they didn't love you. They may have controlled you, used you, been prideful of your accomplishments in public (but abusive about them in private), fed you, clothed you, and given you a home. They may even have told you they loved you and that everything they were doing was for your own good. None of this means they loved you.

When you love someone, how do you treat them? Real love is not punitive; it is accepting. Real love does not control; it guides. Real love applauds in a sincere manner. Real love is there when you are troubled or in pain. Real love sets examples that are healthy. Real love has boundaries and encourages you to have the same.

Make a list of those qualities that you think are the "real love" attributes you would like to have received from your parents. Examples might be: they not only listen to what we have to say, but they hear us; they encourage us to be all that we can be; they tell us verbally and physically (with appropriate affection) that they care and are happy we are in their life. What "real love" qualities did you not get from your parents?

"Real Love" Qualities	Did I Receive or Not?

What you are doing is recreating yourself in the way you would like to have been. In those areas that you felt deficient, you are improving; the areas that were already healthy, you are validating. Your parents may not have given you all the knowledge you needed, but they did the best they could. If your perpetrator was your parent, that is another thing. For them, you make no excuses.

No one is perfect. Your non-abusive parent may have had pressures you weren't aware of. If they themselves were sexually abused, or had early childhood trauma of another nature, and had no opportunity or awareness to work this out, they were incapable of being healthy role models. Cut them some slack as you are hoping to cut yourself slack in the realities you are facing about your own shame.

This is not to say that you are not placing the blame squarely on the perpetrator. As you worked your way through the chapter on Process, you learned to get angry at your perpetrator and make them accountable for everything. You are arriving at an understanding of what really happened, the part everyone played in setting up your future, and the truth of what your life became. Here again, you see so clearly how accountable the perpetrator should have been.

The other side you also see is the clarity of your own unique qualities. Like the sun that comes out from behind the shadows after a storm, you arrive at the truth.

In the realization of this truth, you discover you have never validated these qualities. Make a list. Leave nothing out. Realize that some of these are not new, but have been a part of you for most of your life. As an example: perhaps when you were a child, you were caring and sensitive of other's needs. That very sensitivity may have been the reason why your particular sexual abuse was more painful to you than, say, your neighbor's, who was not very sensitive. Now you can view that quality as a great gift that you have to give others.

My Wonderful Qualities	How Long Have I Had Them?

Take a look at your list. Remind yourself that this is a part to the complete picture that you never saw. You realize you have value. You are a whole person. You have choices. Saying no is easier. Courage develops. With it comes a healthier ego, stronger self-esteem, and wise decisions. You are approaching the end of the bridge. Can you feel the lightning of your heart?

New and exciting things begin to happen. You find, to your surprise, that you enjoy being alone. Prior to getting on that bridge, solitude was a painful choice. Of course it was. Codependency requires other people. Not only that being alone may have meant you'd have to look at truths you'd been running from your whole life. Now that you have validated your own worth, being alone might mean spending time with that one person whose company you enjoy more than anyone, your own. What a marvelous feeling!

Another reward you receive as you approach the end of that bridge happens gradually. When this new world begins to open for you, it will contain that which you never noticed before. The smallest things in life bring joy. It is a joy you were unable to access previously. How can a world filled with chaos and pain present opportunities for abundance? Worse yet, it did. You didn't see them; you didn't care. You had no ability to experience or appreciate any of them. More will be said about this later on in the book, when you will literally learn to "smell the roses".

But first, let's do a very important job. Let's get rid of all your shame. Find a place of peace and strength: a mountain top, a bluff overlooking a river, a meadow, the shore of an ocean. Picture all of your shame, all the negativity you carried for so long. Symbolically place it in a large gunny sack and throw it away. Heave it into the universe once and for all. It was never yours to begin with. All you have done is carry it for others who should have been carrying it themselves.

Another way of doing this is to make your list of shame. Put on some soft music and tear the list to shreds before trashing it. You are not the sum total of what you have done. You are the sum total of who you are, and by now, you recognize that who you are is very special. How do you treat a person who is special? The answer should be clear.

Forgiveness and Confrontation

How does one learn to forgive the unforgivable? Better yet, why should you? It is the greatest challenge you will face as you approach the end of your bridge. Once you understand the concept of negative energy, it is easier to begin forgiving. Once you see that anger turned inward causes physical harm to your body, you will be anxious to feel that healing property called forgiveness.

By now, seeing your family history may have given you insights into why your perpetrator turned out the way he or she did. Understanding is always the key to forgiveness. Not forgiving will hold on to that anger and keep you from healing fully. If you can at least arrive at understanding, it will help.

Remember that forgiving does not in any way mean condoning what your perpetrator has done. They are still responsible and accountable for what they did to you. Webster says forgiveness means, "To give up resentment of or claim to requital for, to cease to feel resentment against." Holding on to resentment and anger is damaging not only to your mental health but to your spiritual, physical, and emotional health as well. Destructive emotion is one of the primary causes of disease. All this means is that you become willing to let it go and start a new life.

If your perpetrator is deceased, it may be easier to do this. For those whose perpetrators are still alive, you may find yourself making the decision that you can no longer be in their presence.

Fig. 7-1: Tossing Out the Shame

This, for those whose perpetrator is a family member, is difficult, if not impossible. How can you possibly move out when you're still in school and economically, if not emotionally, tied to your nuclear family? How difficult it would be to have to avoid that person on a continual basis? Your decision in this area will be one that requires much wisdom. Fortunately, by now, you are almost across that bridge and have arrived at a much healthier and wiser place in your life.

Confronting your perpetrator, especially if it is a parent, is very difficult. But what they are doing is against the law and they can be reported and arrested. For more help with this decision, Google RAINN. This is the Rape, Abuse, and Incest National Network. They not only have a hotline (800-656-HOPE) but can find a local counseling center for you. We all have the right to see who we want to see, to interact with those we choose, even if you are a teenager. Recognizing who is healthy and who is not is one of the things you've learned by now. That gives you the right to put it into practice.

If your perpetrator was a parent, remember there are always friends willing to be substitute mothers and substitute fathers. Find one. You didn't choose your biological parent, but you can choose one now that you willingly give your affection to. You'd be surprised how many people would welcome the opportunity to be an "adopted" parent. Google the organization Big Brothers, Big Sisters. They will match you with an adult who can mentor you and provide the wisdom and support you need in your search for a parental substitute.

Appropriate vs. Inappropriate Affection

One of the most painful things that a sexually molested person has confusion about is what appropriate affection is. You have little wisdom in that area. The pain of your own experience causes red flags to crop up at the sight of any affection between a father and daughter (or mother and son, depending on your own issue). Even if your perpetrator was not a direct family member but another older person in a position of power, you may have moments of discomfort in witnessing certain physical interactions between a child and an older person. This pain can be incredibly intense, not only because fear sets in, but because it flashes pictures from your past you don't want to see. This response is normal.

In trauma, those pictures that lurk in your unconscious, waiting to leap out in present-day events that trigger them, take on more intensity than they deserve. What seems like the pain of current events is often the pain of old stuff. Your emotions run amok, making it difficult to see this. If your intellect tells you that you are overreacting (a common behavior pattern of child sexual abuse victims), then you feel guilt at shaming what may be an innocent interaction.

Physical affection is a marvelous thing to not only watch but experience. Even animals have theirs. But in the life of a person sexually molested, what is a normal, deeply satisfying part of life becomes a minefield. Previous to going through REPAIR, this may have been an issue you were unable to deal with. Hopefully, by the time you arrive at this part, it will be easier. By now, your "trust" issue may be more comfortable to deal with. If this has been a problem in your immediate family, by this part in your program, you should have learned clearer communication skills, giving you the ability to discuss your fears with family members.

Certain guidelines should be kept in mind when you are trying to locate your own comfort zone with affection. Here again, common sense prevails. Tiny infants require different physical affection than a six-year-old, and a six-year-old is comfortable with different affection than an adolescent or teenager. While it may be appropriate to hold that six-year-old on your lap, how appropriate is it for a fifteen-year-old? Remember, your body belongs to you; you can decide who touches it and in what manner.

One of the first questions, and the most important, is whether or not the recipient is comfortable with the affection being given. Teenagers are often not comfortable with the same affection they received when they were younger. It may mean they are going through the transitional stage between child and adult and no longer want to be physical. Clear communication is vital. Set your own boundaries and stick with them.

No parent should ever, once a child is out of diapers and potty-trained, have a reason to poke around in their child's private body parts. As that child grows, they become even more aware of what is private and what is not. A parent checking their child's temperature when they are sick is different from a parent who insists on checking out the size of their teenager's breast development.

With these guidelines and the work you have done thus far in REPAIR, this issue should be less of one. Some things never go away. We all have moments when Father's Day may be a tough one to go through (if your father was your perpetrator). It may resurrect anger and grief, but you will learn to accept that and move through it. You may still have times when seeing a father wrap his arms around a daughter waves that red flag. But now, you can put that action in the right perspective and deal with it. While these new behavior patterns and responses don't happen overnight, they do happen.

John Bradshaw talks about the one-legged ice skater he saw in Toronto. Will you ever regain your leg? No. Will you learn how to skate? Yes. Keeping this in mind will give you balance.

You have discovered that you must crawl before walking, walk before running. *Running sets you free.* Now you are ready to arrive at the concept of Rhythm. It is one of the most exciting concepts you will ever discover and opens a world you never thought to access. You are ready to step off the bridge onto the shore beyond.

Rhythm

The ending of recovery
Is the beginning of the rest of your life—

The way it was meant to be.

The path you took in life and the decisions you made at the crossroads were shaped by your experiences. As a child of sexual abuse, those experiences were a horror most people cannot imagine. Nor would they want to. People who were free to become all they wanted to be cannot know what it is like to live in a prison. In completing this program, you are releasing yourself from that prison.

Once you are free, you begin to return to one of the greatest joys all living creatures have— their own rhythm. Even animals have their own rhythm and would fight mightily against anyone who tried to take it away. If you go back far enough, you can remember waking at the same time every morning and getting tired at the same time every night. You had a time for hunger, a time for energy, and a time for languor. Being a part of that natural rhythm brought joy as well as serenity. Life, predictable and comfortable, contained meaning and purpose. It was like a dance, one where you moved freely through your own universe, bending and swaying your body in time to your inner voices.

A newborn child has its own rhythm. They sleep through feedings or are constantly hungry; they eat at six-hour intervals instead of four; they cry a lot or they're quiet. They respond to Uncle Jake who has a delightful sense of play, or they cry when Grandma Benton with her loud, shrill voice comes into the room. They are already their own unique personality with no one in the world quite like them. Their rhythm is not right or wrong, only different, but it is theirs. Your rhythm may be the only thing that is truly yours.

As a child of trauma, your natural rhythm was interrupted. Sexual violation shattered the serenity of your early rhythm. A child violated at the age of one has already established a natural rhythm. Once molested, the older the child grows, the more unnatural adaptations are made to their own rhythm. They hide their intense emotions out of fear of punishment and a parent's rage. When laughing at the dinner table sends them to their bedroom without food, they learn to contain their sense of humor and playfulness. Building tunnels in the living room out of blankets and chairs, a marvelous example of a child's creative nature, causes Mom to go into a fit of anger over the mess. The child learns to stifle their creativity.

As the years go by, out of a sense of fear, rejection, and feeling "less than", the real person hides deeper and deeper until once into adulthood, little remains of that spontaneous, childlike human. The mask they wear contains a great deal of anger. Who wants to be somber when your nature flows with joy? Why pretend you are submissive when being strong-minded is the real you? Holding your body stiff when you inwardly crave hugs is a sad, almost anguishing part of so many humans.

Natural rhythm is just that—natural. It is the essence of who and what you are. Being able to return to it is freeing as well as strengthening. As was clearly illustrated earlier, you had gifts of awareness that could have enabled you to be and have whatever you wanted. All the tools for a happy life were taken away by the childhood sexual abuse. At birth, you had potential for the inner strength needed to deal with life's problems. As a sexually molested child, you lost it.

Let's talk about inner strength for a moment. Have you ever envied someone who appears "strong as a rock"? Have you ever wished that someone was you? With the proper application of this program, it can be. Inner strength is like a shield you wear to protect you from the trials life presents. There is no way you can avoid these trials, but you can program yourself to make choices that will minimize them and think of solutions that will deal effectively with them. After REPAIR, you'll be able to handle any grief that might come into your life by moving through the healthy stages from denial to anger to guilt to depression, and finally to acceptance.

Strong people have the ability to make not only wise choices about the direction of their life, but also have the courage to take those steps. Strong people are not afraid of the truth and can apologize when wrong without feeling shame. Remember, a strong person is not always big, but a big person is always strong. Strong people can survive the day-to-day problems as well as the traumatizing ones that come out of nowhere.

We're not talking about those who are stubborn. There's a big difference. Stubborn people are inflexible; strong people are not. Stability is a quality that all wounded children crave. Ridding ourselves of that shaking in the heart and that confusion in the mind that is a result of childhood trauma seems like an unattainable goal to one who has been molested. As you moved through this program, you began to grow. With growth comes a steadying of your own course as well as strengthening of your inner self. If you worked a rigorous Twelve-Step Program, you learned about flexibility and honesty. You also learned about change.

Life is about change. Changing those things that are appropriate is part of gaining confidence. Refusing to change them will almost guarantee the continuing of low self-esteem. On the other hand, keeping those qualities that are uniquely yours, the appropriate ones, is part of your natural rhythm. You don't want anything more taken away from you. You have lost enough already.

Guidelines to acquiring wisdom—and thereby strength—are simple. The golden rule—*Do unto others as you would have them do unto you*—still works best. Even spiritual beliefs, as opposed to rigid religious guidelines, should be founded on this. As you approach the end of your bridge, you will make the marvelous discovery that most of the old adages are true. *A Stitch in time, saves nine; Watch the pennies and the dollars will take care of themselves* will resurrect to give you wisdom. Take a hard look at all those you're aware of. Utilize what you have learned thus far to keep the good ones and discard the foolish. *Children should be seen and not heard* is an incredibly stupid statement. Our mothers would have done better to have said, *The spontaneous but disciplined child is a happy child.*

One has only to watch nature to see the importance of following your own rhythm. As the seasons change, so does that rhythm. If you follow the path of nature, you can see that rhythm is inherent in all things of God. A plant grows from a seed into a sapling, into a trunk with branches, and then bears blossoms and fruit. It has a time to shrivel and die and yet another time to be reborn. Everything in the land has a rhythm. And so it is with humans. Take a walk in a forest and observe Mother Nature. There are more truths and wisdom hidden in her depths than anywhere in the world.

As you emerge on the other side of the Bridge of Recovery, you will begin to crave your own blueprint (rhythm), the one you originally had. You will want order instead of chaos. You will think ahead rather than act on impulse. You will work through challenges knowing that when something distressing happens, *the only thing that's the end of the world is the end of the world.*

Toxic people and toxic excitement will now feel like instability and insanity. What is even more gratifying is your ability to recognize these things. The discomfort acquired from being in the presence of toxicity will prompt you to arrange your life in a rhythm that not only brings serenity but predictability. Predictability is not synonymous with boredom. A need for excitement through partying, arguing, drugs, alcohol, and multiple sex partners will now seem immature and dangerous in your newly established world of peace. The natural high you have heard people speak of will become a part of your life.

Everyone's rhythm is unique. Are you a morning person or an evening person? Are you hungry when you first awaken or is your appetite not stimulated until you've been up and about for hours? Do you like quiet or do you like noise? Are material possessions a need or are you Spartan? Do you fancy travel or do you like to be rooted? Are you a talker or a listener? Is your humor quiet or are you raucous and rowdy?

None of these are right or wrong, just different. We cannot all be the same and if you try to bend a branch, so that it will grow in a direction contrary to its nature, it will wither and die. So it is that you must be true to your own inner self and become a part of your innate natural rhythm.

A sense of freedom develops once you become true to your own nature. Shakespeare proclaimed: *To thine own self be true*. His words ring with truth. When you are forced to do what is opposite to your natural rhythm, resentment sets in. Stemming from what you perceive as a wrong or injury, it digs its own hole. Most of the time, such an emotion begins with a lack of honesty.

If you tell a friend you don't mind baby-sitting their children, when in fact you were looking forward to attending a play, resentment settles in. You are not helping your friend or yourself by this lack of honesty. Maybe taking care of children is not your area of expertise. Perhaps suggesting another friend to baby-sit while you offer to take your friend to a play is more in line with your own rhythm. Why pretend to be what you are not? Assertiveness and honesty are needed to combat resentment.

This does not mean that it is okay to do whatever you feel like, regardless of consequences; it means tempering your real nature with common sense. Laugher is vital, but is it appropriate during a church sermon or at the expense of someone else's emotional wellbeing? A healthy sense of discipline is important as well as a sense of fair play. Indulging oneself in strong opinions and being single-minded of purpose is admirable. How admirable does it become when you hurt others as a result of it? Have you ever heard the parents of an only child who is tearing your house apart make the comment, *"Isn't he cute? He's a natural born leader."*? What's missing in this picture?

Children who have been sexually abused, as well as all wounded children, begin wearing masks at an early age. Afraid to be who they really are, they choose different masks for different encounters. That way, no one has to see their true selves. Filled with shame from childhood trauma, they don't see themselves as jewels, and slipping on the mask enables them to not only hide from their real selves but escape another's disappointment or wrath.

After you go through recovery and begin locating those treasures that were always there, your self-esteem builds. This gives you courage to throw away the masks. Once the real you steps out, being unrestrained presents rapture you could scarcely imagine prior to recovery.

A good example of those who followed their own rhythm is that of our forefathers. They knew what they were doing when they journeyed across the waters to a new land. Deprived of the right to worship in the manner of their own choice, they set out to find a place where they could be themselves. In turning their backs on tyranny, they were setting boundaries as well as following dreams and goals. They knew they had choices, and coming to a land where they could explore them was the first step to individuality. Fortunately, they had the wisdom to understand that not everyone's choice was the same. Thus the United States became a land of multiple religions as well as one of tolerance and acceptance.

Feeling accepted is necessary. As a child of trauma, you only experienced acceptance when you were obedient to your parents and the world outside. While at times, obedience was a necessary ingredient in making your way into adulthood, often it required limiting your choices and wearing masks that covered up the real person—literally, the inner child.

Once you complete recovery, your own rhythm will begin to form. Natural behavior patterns will emerge. As layer upon layer of your true self comes together, in time, you will realize that this is what you have craved since the trauma.

For a teenager still living at home, becoming your own person may create a problem. If you have parents who are supportive of the REPAIR program you are working, they will understand and applaud your newly acquired wisdom about being who you really are. But if one of your parents is your perpetrator, you are back to what was discussed in the previous chapter. What they are doing is against the law and they can be arrested. Contact RAINN and seek counseling as to how to handle this. As you've been traveling across that bridge, your personality has been changing. By now, your family members will be well aware of what is happening. You may have some who are supportive and some who are not. Teenagers have the right to healthy choices and if your parents are not comfortable with this, you need to seek the help of a counselor and/or contact RAINN.

Picture waking up in a world where all of the choices are your own. Remember the cartoon of the woman in the three-sided cage. You have stepped out of yours into a world of freedom. It is impossible, once you cross that bridge, to remain in an unhealthy environment. Now your entire day will pulsate with your own rhythm. Now you can turn all the mountains into rocks, the rocks into pebbles.

Fig. 8-1: Mountains into Rocks, Rocks into Pebbles, ...

Do the following exercise to return to what you really are. Describe your natural rhythm in the following areas:

(i.e., I sleep deep or light, I snore, I hug pillows, I'm a fast talker, rowdy humor etc.)

Sleeping _____

_____

_____

Conversation _____

_____

_____

Humor _____

_____

_____

Hobbies and interests _____

_____

_____

_____

My favorite people would look like:_____

_____

_____

My favorite foods are: _____

_____

_____

_____

My value system includes: _____

_____

_____

_____

My political affiliation and beliefs are: _____

_____

_____

_____

My religious and spiritual beliefs and needs are: _____

_____

_____

_____

List other areas of your life, your likes and dislikes. Show a clear picture of those things with which you are most comfortable. How many are in your life now? Why are the others not?

Do not be uncomfortable with the fact that your rhythm is different than your siblings, your friends, or your parents. The world would be a boring place if we were all the same. Not only that, there would be no progress. It is only in our individuality that we begin discovery, and discovery is one of the most vital parts of a world that moves in harmony.

The more you choose to follow the path of your own nature, the happier you'll be. As always, this guideline must be tempered with wisdom. The ability to use common sense as a tool to navigate through life is invaluable. Unfortunately, the only thing wrong is it isn't very common—one of the reasons the world is in such a tangle. Some of the basic rules are:

- Do that which works.
- If it's not broken, don't fix it.
- Let sleeping dogs lie.
- Respond, don't react.
- Choose your battles wisely
- Use your head before using your words.

How many others can you think of? Using common sense as well as staying within your own rhythm brings stability and serenity.

By now you probably see the senselessness of being judgmental. Because of the pain you carried at such a young age, the ability to accept shortcomings in others (and here we're not talking about abuse) became criticism and harsh judgments instead. Unable to look at your own behavior because of the fear that you may not like what you see, you looked at others. In the process of REPAIRing, you came to see that not only did you learn to recognize and love the real you, but in doing so, you no longer had a reason to judge others. Judgments carry a heavy load. You have discovered that just because they're yours doesn't make them gospel—only the gospel according to you. With Twelve-Steppers, the need to be judgmental is often softened by rephrasing it as "righteous indignation". This lends a certain humor to whatever you find not okay about another person.

Judgments are also negative. Hopefully, you have been so busy improving yourself that you have had no time to judge others. That too brings a lightening of your load. Like a sailing ship in a race, you want to throw everything overboard that is weighing you down. Only in this will you have a better chance of finding your own rhythm.

You have been discarding a belief system handed you by your parents; one that was not really yours. One of the rewards of recovery is a fine-tuning of *your* value system. Once you perceive what is true and what is not, it will be easy to incorporate these into your life. This too makes you feel a part of your natural rhythm.

Now, the world opens up for you. You see possibilities you never thought of. If previously you only reacted to events that life presents, now you can respond. In addition, you can begin to seek out your dreams. Unencumbered with the pain of your childhood trauma, moving ahead will be your primary goal.

Once you have worked your way through recovery, you will find no need to dredge up things from the past. You may always be aware of what happened, but like a wound that has been lanced, drained of its infection, and healed with only a scar, you seldom are even aware of the scar. And the few times it comes into your mind, you recognize it as such—only a scar.

Now that you have completed the stages of REPAIR, you are ready to find out about post recovery.

Post Recovery

How do you know when it's time to leave this world?

When you stop learning.

Post recovery, the stage that hangs around after you complete your REPAIR program, therapy, and your Twelve-Step Program, (depending on whether you utilize all three or not) is an often neglected and fragile time. By now you've learned the tools, but you haven't necessarily used all of them. When do you arrive at this stage? Sometimes step number twelve dovetails with other events in your life. It might be when you finally step away from an abusive or unhealthy relationship. Or maybe the final step gives you the courage to find a part-time job to establish your independence or begin making plans for college. Whatever happens, it will bring monumental changes—all for the better.

If you are seeing a counselor, when will you be ready to discontinue therapy? Only you, with the help of your therapist, will know. Hopefully you have been listening to your inner voices and will have developed a stronger self-esteem. Along with that comes the confidence and the courage to live your own life. It's an exciting time. Your own rhythm has been established and you are in the process of finding even more of your own unique behavior patterns. It's amazing how much confidence you feel during this period.

Then comes a test, that first time when you make a choice and it turns out to be not so wise. It may be a failed relationship that, in your new flush of excitement, you rushed into, only to see it come crashing about you. It may be a change in your part-time job that turned out to be not as wonderful as you had thought. Confusion and frustration take over. What went wrong? You thought recovery was supposed to help you find the pot of gold at the end of the rainbow. Didn't you do it right?

One of the results of recovery and a strong self-esteem is the ability to understand and develop a sense of personal responsibility. This acceptance of your own foibles not only makes them feel less upsetting, but places an objectivity needed to find your way out of whatever mess you find yourself in. Your friends will find it an endearing and courageous trait.

Beating yourself up is an old behavior pattern. Recognize it as such. No one is perfect. If you don't believe this, pull out the morning's newspaper and read it.

You'll find so many people making so many mistakes that it will put yours in the right perspective. Pat yourself on the back for having the insight to recognize you "did wrong" and the courage to "do right". Find humor in the situation and in no time, you'll be telling your friends about the hole you stepped in and how you so adeptly stepped back out.

Old behavior patterns do not change overnight. Depending on the behavior, the addiction, and the severity of the original trauma, the average number of years to totally rid yourself of addictive type behavior is two to five. Do not be alarmed if you slip in your resolve to make only healthy choices. Now is not the time to spiral back into hopelessness. Take a deep breath; find some quiet time to listen to your inner voices; and remember the Tenth Step—*We continued to take personal inventory and when we were wrong, promptly admitted it.* That's what the steps are for. They are your friends, your mentors, and all you need do to find your balance is read them over one more time. Another great tool is the serenity prayer: *God grant me the serenity to accept the things I cannot change, the courage to change the things I can, and the wisdom to know the difference.* Be forgiving of yourself when you make a mistake or slip back into old behavior patterns. Whether it's a relapse or a temporary glitch depends on inner self-talk.

Pull out your by-now-worn copy of REPAIR and locate the section on help in the middle of your journey. Go back and read your magic mirror. It is not a good idea to dismantle it immediately; you'll need it in the months to come. If you've done the program right, you'll discover that you now have the tools to handle these little speed bumps in life. Take refresher courses now and then with a seminar on self-esteem, a new book or recording you've heard about, or just going back and listening to the old ones. When you become shaky, it's helpful to get reinforcement from the original sources that got you on the right track. You'll bounce back in no time, eventually discovering that what seemed like poor choices were in fact tests that, rather than weakening you, will strengthen you. Facing fear brings strength and lessens the fear.

Taking life one day at a time is important. All you really have is the present anyway. If you do some planning, use your head, and listen to your inner voices, taking life one day at a time will come automatically. Turning any large worries over to your Higher Power helps. Twelve-Steppers talk about turning problems over and then grabbing them back. The need to control your own environment is one you keep slipping back into. All you learned may feel like a double-edged sword. Aren't you supposed to take charge of your own life? Use the serenity prayer as a guide.

Another guideline is a reality check. If what you're trying to control is your stuff, that's one thing. But if it's another person's, leave it alone. Why would you want to take on another's opportunities for growth? In doing so, you not only deprive them of the joy of growing in that area, but distract yourself from your own growth. Once you've gone through a few tests, you'll find that the challenges are not so difficult to overcome, and as time goes by, you'll have fewer.

For many years, you followed a certain path. That path contained responses that got you in a lot of trouble. Now you've learned new and better responses, but they too will take time to develop until they become automatic. We are creatures of habit. Be patient.

In taking life one day at a time, you'll also enjoy it more. All the things you didn't notice previously—sunsets and sunrises, the smile on a child's face, new recipes in the Food Section of your paper, a friendly neighbor who offers a hand, and the smell of new mown grass—will now be daily occurrences. You'll learn to savor the moments. This is the way life was meant to be. Abundance will follow your days, accompanied by a feeling of finding the calm in the center of any storm that, prior to recovery, seemed far beyond your reach.

Previously you may have been so codependent that only in the company of others did you feel comfortable. Now that you've worked your way through REPAIR and have discovered your own wonderfulness, you'll realize the joy of solitude. When you thought you had no value, there was little interest in being alone. At times, it was terrifying. Only outside distractions kept you from having to face that reality. Your new-found desire to enjoy your own company will not only give you a feeling of being centered, it will decrease your anxiety about not having a significant other. In time, you'll see that if one comes along, you'll be ready; if not, you're so busy having a great time by yourself that it won't matter. This is not to say that if finding someone to grow old with is part of your dream, you should give it up. You can still make yourself available to meet new people. But once you do, you won't feel so frantic about it, and an even greater blessing occurs; you'll pull in healthier people. John Bradshaw talks about the woman who kept getting date-raped and when asked where she went to meet men, responded, *biker bars*. You will no longer be tempted to go to a biker bar or anywhere else where you meet the wrong kind of person.

As you learn to set new boundaries, others will respect them. Those who don't will wander off to find a more willing victim. An unhealthy person cannot survive long in a healthy environment and vice versa.

Now that you've eliminated your negativity and are surrounding yourself with optimism, you'll be surprised how different your world will be. Doors will open, parking spaces vacate, solutions to problems jump in front of you, and new people will come into your life to enhance it and further your own causes. Positive energy attracts positive and negative energy pulls in negative. Unhealthy people will no longer want to be near you. That's great! And your new-found confidence will pull in winners.

Now you can set your mind to other things. One of the most important is learning about goal setting. You have the rest of your life in front of you. What do you want to do with it—especially now that you know how to make healthy choices?

Pretend that everything you want is yours for the asking. Then make a list of all of them. Leave nothing off. Why not dream big? If you're not sure what direction you want to head into, do some research. Brainstorm your interests. Are you happy with your elective classes at school? Why not? What would you like to take instead? If you're starting to feel attraction to a certain career, how would you get there? Be realistic. If you can't hold a tune and always wanted to be a world famous opera singer, that may be outside your reach. But in a world filled with potential, there must be something that is not. Some occupations—writing, for example—age can only improve.

Explore ideas; follow threads; go to a bookstore and see what interests attract you. Do more writing, more brain-storming. Talk to friends who are accomplishing goals and ask them how they're doing it. Many motivational media and books are available. Remember that repetitive listening is the key.

There is not only a solution for every problem, there is an adventure for every boredom. Auntie Mame, in the novel of the same name by Patrick Dennis, said, *Life is a banquet and most poor suckers are starving to death.* What would you like at your banquet and why are you going hungry?

Take a look at all aspects of your life. Then write down whether or not you are satisfied with them. If not, write down possible changes you could make. Use the following exercise as a guideline:

Personal relationships: ____Satisfied ____Not Satisfied

What I can do to change it? _____

_____

Career or School Choice: ____Satisfied ____Not Satisfied

What I can do to change it? _____

_____

Residence: ____Satisfied ____Not Satisfied

What I can do to change it? _____

_____

Hobbies and Interests: ____Satisfied ____Not Satisfied

What I can do to change them? _____

List other aspects of your life and ways to change them.

_____

_____

_____

_____

_____

Now make the following lists:

Things I always wished I could do but never did:

_____

_____

_____

_____

Ways I can accomplish each one of them:

_____

_____

_____

_____

Not everyone's world is perfect after recovery. Life goes on, and sometimes it contains heartache and challenges. There will be deaths and financial stress; you may not find the man/woman of your dreams, and so on. But in your pre-recovery days, when these things happened, it felt like the end of the world. Now you know it never was. Now you're better equipped to take things in stride. Move through the challenges, keeping in mind that every one faced head-on brings strength and purpose. *An easy task becomes difficult when done with reluctance.* Don't face life with reluctance; face it with purpose and courage. Most people die without ever having lived their dreams. At the end of the time allotted to you, the only thing you'll regret is the things you didn't do that you wanted to. Make bold moves and make every one count.

This is different from reacting. This is about thinking things through, coming up with choices, and making the appropriate ones with courage. This is about making your life the way you'd like it to be. You've been in basic training and have earned the right to be all that you can be.

Let's talk about purpose, that path in life you were meant to be on. Everyone has one, but not everyone has the ability to recognize it. The fulfillment of purpose is one of life's greatest joys. Are you any clearer about your purpose? What would you like it to be? Are you a flower child who would like to relax and enjoy? That's fine too. The important thing is to be happy and enjoy life— our God-given right at birth. You've been sidetracked from it for too long.

*   *   *

One of the biggest benefits in reaching the other side of the bridge is an awareness of your physical health. While living on the dark side, concern about your physical wellbeing rated low on your list of interests. Once you've faced the demons from your past and learned to avoid stepping in the same destructive holes, you're going to take a keen interest in living a long life.

This means changing lifestyle habits in diet, exercise, and other preventive medicine areas. Here follows a few words to guide you through these.

Diet

Invest in a class on Nutrition. It may save your life. At the very least, take a look at the books, websites, and apps available on the subject. Subscribe to health promotion magazines and steep yourself in information on what to eat. If your school has classes in diet and nutrition, take them. Like recovery, information on good nutrition is everywhere. If you follow the guidelines of the Food Pyramid for a period of only one week, you will notice a substantial difference in your emotional wellbeing.

Exercise

Begin a daily regime of exercise. Check out exercise videos; walk thirty minutes each day; find a local gym; or start bicycling. Decide on whatever exercise you like. This will accomplish more than one purpose. You'll meet new people of similar interests, and with the addition of good nutrition, the results in your emotional stability will be dramatic.

Dental Care

When is the last time you had your teeth checked? How good are you at flossing and regular brushing? Do you really want false teeth by the age of 50? Ask your parents if you can schedule a checkup with a dentist. If you've been seeing one but not following any suggestions, put yourself on a regular program of good dental hygiene.

Addictive Negative Habits

If you smoke, you may finally have the courage to quit. Smoking is sometimes a way of distracting yourself from the pain of that inner child. Once you bring happiness to that child, she won't need a cigarette in her hand to cope. Since you're now living in a new world, make it a healthy one. If you've had an alcohol problem, hopefully you joined AA For Teens and can now prevent any leanings in that department taking one day at a time and going to meetings.

Good Grooming

One who looks good, feels good. How long have you been telling yourself you're going to get a new hairdo or start doing a regular manicure? You don't need to spend a lot of money to begin taking care of the cosmetic side to your body. A simple foot massage after a bubble bath in the evening is a way of pampering yourself with good grooming (these are for the girls). Take more care with your makeup; find more stylish and flattering ways to dress. If you have a few pounds that need to disappear, you're more apt to do this in the post-recovery period. Are you paying attention to little things that girls notice like bad breath from irregular brushings, not using mouthwash etc. There are loads of ways to prevent this problem. Guys need to pay more attention to their grooming habits and what they're wearing as well.

* * *

I hope REPAIR has proven beneficial in changing your life and am grateful for the opportunity to help you on your journey. The things you have learned in this program are life-changing tools. Avail yourself of them on a daily basis. You have finally recognized that the most important person in your world is you, a whole new you, one who is going to be a part of all the wonderful things waiting on the other side of that bridge.

Appendix - Resources

The Desiderata by Max Ehrmann

"Go placidly amidst the noise and haste and remember what peace there may be in silence. As far as possible, without surrender, be on good terms with all persons. Speak your truth quietly and clearly and listen to others, even the dull and ignorant for they too have their story. Avoid loud and aggressive persons, for they are vexations to the spirit.

If you compare yourself with others you may become vain or bitter; for always there will be greater and lesser persons than yourself. Enjoy your achievements as well as your plans. Keep interested in your own career, how-ever humble; it is a real possession in the changing fortunes of time.

Exercise caution in your business affairs; for the world is full of trickery. But let this not blind you to what virtue there is; many people strive for high ideals; and every-where life is full of heroism. Be yourself. Especially, do not feign affection. Neither be cynical about love; for in the face of all aridity and disenchantment it is perennial as the grass.

Take kindly the counsel of the years, gracefully sur-rendering things of youth. Nurture strength of spirit to shield you in sudden misfortune. But do not distress yourself with imaginings. Many fears are born of fatigue and loneliness.

Beyond a wholesome discipline, be gentle with your-self. You are a child of the universe, no less than the trees and the stars; you have a right to be here. And whether or not it is clear to you, no doubt the universe is unfolding as it should.

Therefore be at peace with God, whatever you conceive Him to be, and whatever your labors and aspirations, in the noisy confusion of life keep peace with your soul.

With all its sham, drudgery and broken dreams, it is still a beautiful world. Be careful. Strive to be happy."

The Twelve Steps

1) We admitted we were powerless over others and that our lives had become unmanageable.

2) Came to believe that a power greater than ourselves could restore us to sanity.

3) Made a decision to turn our lives over to the care of God as we understood God.

4) Made a fearless and searching moral inventory of ourselves.

5) Admitted to God, to ourselves, and to another human being the exact nature of our wrongs.

6) Were entirely ready to have God remove all these defects of character.

7) Humbly asked God to remove our shortcomings.

8) Made a list of people we had harmed and became willing to make amends to them all.

9) Made direct amends wherever possible, except when to do so would harm themselves or others.

10) Continued to take personal inventory and when we were wrong, promptly admitted it.

11) Sought through prayer and meditation to improve our conscious contact with God, praying only for knowledge of his will and the power to carry it out.

12) Having had a spiritual awakening as a result of these steps, we tried to carry this message to others and to practice these principles in all our affairs.

THE SERENITY PRAYER

God

grant me the serenity

to accept the things

I cannot change,

the courage

to change the things I can,

and the wisdom to know

the difference.

The Ten Promises

I Promise

To be so strong that nothing can disturb my peace of mind.

To talk health, happiness, and prosperity to every person I meet.

To make all my friends feel there is something special in them.

To look at the sunny side of everything and make my optimism come true.

To think only of the best, to work only for the best, and expect only the best.

To be just as enthusiastic about the success of others as I am about my own.

To forget the mistakes of the past and press on to the greater achievement of the future.

To wear a cheerful countenance at all times and give every living creature I meet a smile.

To give so much time to the improvement of myself that I have no time to criticize or judge others.

To be too large for worry, too noble for anger, too strong for fear, and too happy to permit the presence of trouble.

From *Your Forces and How to Use Them* by Christian D. Larson (1912).

Support Groups, Sites, and Reading List

For all Twelve-Step Programs

For the phone number of the Twelve-Step Program you want in your area, call 1-800-555-1212. Ask for the Program of your choice and the phone number to the area in which you live.

Some of the major Twelve-Step Programs are:

- Alcoholics Anonymous
- Al-Anon
- Codependents Anonymous
- Overeaters Anonymous
- Narcotics Anonymous

Join the Lamplighter Movement at www.thelamplighters.org. Check it out to see if there is a Lamplighter chapter near you. If not, you might want to start one yourself. It is so easy. The details are all on the website.

Websites

www.catharsisfoundation.org Catharsis Foundation is a non-profit incorporated in Calgary Alberta in 2004 for survivors of ALL forms of child abuse—internationally

www.thelamplighters.org The Lamplighters is a movement founded by Marjorie McKinnon, author of *REPAIR Your Life*, for survivors of incest and child sexual abuse. Emphasizes the importance of REPAIRing the damage done and recommends using the program REPAIR as a model for recovery.

www.angelashelton.com Angela Shelton is a public speaker, author, actress, writer and advocate for victims of child sexual abuse.

www.mskinnermusic.com Mike Skinner offers Hope, Healing & Help for Trauma, Abuse & Mental Health through music, resources and advocacy

www.preventchildabuse.org Since 1972, *Prevent Child Abuse America* has led the way in building awareness, providing education and inspiring hope to everyone involved in the effort to prevent the abuse and neglect of our nation's children.

www.rainn.org *The Rape, Abuse & Incest National Network* is the nation's largest anti-sexual assault organization and has been ranked as one of "America's 100 Best Charities" by *Worth* magazine.

www.recoverybooks.com The recovery and self-help bookstore.

www.prevent-abuse-now.com This website, also called *Pandora's Box* offers information, offenses, prevention and protection regarding child sexual abuse.

www.selfesteemshop.com The most comprehensive collection of self-help books for abuse recovery you'll find anywhere.

www.stopcsa.org The goal of *Stop The Silence* is to stop child sexual abuse and related forms of violence by changing societal relationships among and between groups.

www.darkness2light.org *Darkness to Light* is a national nonprofit organization and initiative that seeks to diminish the incidence and impact of child sexual abuse, so that more children will grow up healthy and whole

Reading List - Recovery

Barth, A. (2009). *101 tips for survivors of sexual abuse: A pocket book of wisdom.* Ann Arbor, MI: Loving Healing Press

Barth, A., & Kinra, R. (2009). *Annabelle's secret: A story about sexual abuse.* Ann Arbor, MI: Loving Healing Press

Bass, E., & Davis, L. (1988). *The courage to heal: A guide for women survivors of child sexual abuse.* New York: Perennial Library

Bean, B., & Bennett, S. (1997). *The me nobody knows: A guide for teen survivors.* San Francisco: Jossey-Bass Publishers

Dessen, S. (2006). *Just listen: A novel.* New York: Viking Children's Books

Gloeckner, P. (2002). *Diary of a teenage girl: An account in words and pictures.* Berkeley, Calif: Frog.

Jeffers, S. (2006). *Feel the fear and do it anyway.* New York: Ballantine.

Lerner, H. (2005). *The dance of anger: a woman's guide to changing the patterns of intimate relationships.* New York: Harper.

Marcy-Webster, S., & Phillips, E. (2006). *If I tell.* Indianapolis, IN: KIDSRIGHTS

Munson, L., Riskin, K., & Child Welfare League of America. (1995). *In their own words: A sexual abuse workbook for teenage girls.* Washington, DC: Child Welfare League of America.

Mather, C. L., & Debye, K. E. (1994). *How long does it hurt?: A guide to recovering from incest and sexual abuse for teenagers, their friends, and their families.* San Francisco: Jossey-Bass.

Reading List - Therapists & Caregivers

Berman, P. (1994). *Therapeutic exercises for victimized and neglected girls: Applications for individual, family, and group psychotherapy.* Sarasota, Fla: Professional Resource Press.

Gil, E. (1996). *Treating abused adolescents.* New York: Guilford Press.

Krill, W. E. (2011). *Gentling: A practical guide to treating PTSD in abused children.* Ann Arbor, MI: Loving Healing Press

Volkman, M. K. (2007). *Children and traumatic incident reduction: Creative and cognitive approaches*. Ann Arbor, MI: Loving Healing Press

Reading List - Post-Recovery

Chopra, D., (1994). *The seven spiritual laws of success: A practical guide to the fulfillment of your dreams*. San Rafael, Calif: Amber-Allen Pub.

Frankl, V. E., (1963). *Man's search for meaning: An Introduction to Logotheraphy*. New York: Pocket Books

Hammarskjo ld, D., et al (1964). *Markings*. New York: Knopf.

Lindbergh, A. M., & Pforzheimer, C. H. (1955). *Gift from the sea*. New York: Pantheon.

Mazari, N., & Hillman, R. (2008). *The rugmaker of Mazar-e-Sharif*. Elsternwick, Vic: Insight Publications.

McWilliams, P., & John-Roger. (1989). *You can't afford the luxury of a negative thought*. Los Angeles, Calif: Prelude Press

Moore, T. (1992). *Care of the soul: A guide for cultivating depth and sacredness in everyday life*. New York, NY: HarperCollins

Moore, T. (1994). *Soul mates: Honoring the mysteries of love and relationship*. New York, NY: HarperPerennial.

McKinnon, M. (2011). *It's your choice!: Decisions that will change your life*. Ann Arbor, MI: Loving Healing Press.

Volkman, M. K. (2005). *Life skills: Improve the quality of your life with metapsychology*. Ann Arbor, Mich: Loving Healing Press.

A Suggested List of Audio Media - Recovery

Bradshaw, John, *The Family*

Bradshaw, John, *Healing The Shame That Binds You*

Beattie, Melody, *Codependent No More*

Beattie, Melody, *Beyond Codependency*

A Suggested List of Audio Media - Post-Recovery

Bradshaw, John, *Creating Love*

Bradshaw, John, *The Next Great Stage of Growth*

Canfield, Jack, *Self Esteem and Peak Performance*

Peale, Norman Vincent, *The Power of Positive Thinking*

Peale, Norman Vincent, *Positive Imaging*

Robbins, Anthony, *Unlimited Power*

Ziglar, Zig, Goals: *Setting & Achieving Them on Schedule*

These lists are only suggestive and not, by any means, the only ones available. Your local bookstore and library contain a wealth of recovery books and discs.

About the Author

In 1988, prompted by severe depression and resurfacing memories, Marjorie McKinnon entered a program for recovery from incest, a journey that took almost five years to complete. During that time, she wrote about her experience, a chronicle of going from a place of despair to one of joy. That book, titled *Let Me Hurt You and Don't Cry Out* was her first attempt to get published.

Unable to sell it, she spent the next five years developing a program on recovery from child sexual abuse. Despite being a non-professional, it was her belief that a program devised by someone who had walked the same road would be a sensitive and pragmatic resource. She titled that self-published book, *REPAIR: A Program for Recovery from Incest & Childhood Sexual Abuse* and used it as an accompaniment to seminars she taught in the Los Angeles area.

In the last ten years, Marjorie has completed a fiction trilogy that follows the life of Kathleen McGuire whose spirit guide, Jake, provides her with wisdom and direction from another world as she gets herself in and out of trouble. Three nonfiction works, *Mystical Experiences: Tales of The Inner Light, Blue Skies and Green Lights: How to Create a Perfect World Through Positive Growth in The Six Dimensions,* a post-recovery book, and *A Common Sense Spiritual Path,* as well as a mystery novel, *When First We Practice to Deceive* and a fiction work titled: *Here Lies,* are all completed. *Hello, My Name is Marjorie,* close to completion, is a sprightly and often humorous email account of her courtship with Tom McKinnon, her husband, whom she met on the Internet while doing genealogy research for the McKinnon clan (her name was also McKinnon). Another novel, *After The Rain,* and a nonfiction work called, *Our Greatest Asset: The Elderly* are works in progress.

Marjorie is currently doing speaking engagements in the northern Arizona area and is the founder of *The Lamplighters,* a movement for victims of child sexual abuse that emphasizes the importance of REPAIRing the damage. Feeling that a movement of one voice would give more power to survivors, she hopes one day to have Lamplighters all over the world. Currently, there are 32 chapters in 21 states, one chapter in Tokyo, Japan, two in Ontario, Canada and one in Plymouth, England. The interest in people wanting to start chapters is daily. If you would like to find the nearest one or consider starting your own chapter, then please take a few moments to visit the Lamplighter's website: http://TheLamplighters.org.

Index

CPSIA information can be obtained at www.ICGtesting.com
Printed in the USA
BVOW081647090512

289826BV00005B/1/P